Computer Netw

Crucial Study Texts for Computing Degree Courses

Titles in the series

Computer Networks

Philip J Irving

**Computing series editor:
Peter Hodson**

Dedication

This book is dedicated to the important people in my life who made this all possible: Elizabeth, Victoria Rose, Philip, Margaret, Frank, Ena, Pat and Keith. Thanks for your help and support. Special thanks to Rob for his critical eye and Peter for his support.

First published in 2003 by Crucial, a division of Learning Matters Ltd.

British Library Cataloguing in Publication Data
A CIP record for this book is available from the British Library.

ISBN 1 903337 06 2

Cover design by Topics – The Creative Partnership
Project management by Deer Park Productions
Text design by Code 5 Design
Printed and bound by Bell & Bain Ltd, Glasgow

Learning Matters Ltd
33 Southernhay East
Exeter EX1 1NX
Tel: 01392 215560
Email: info@learningmatters.co.uk
www.learningmatters.co.uk

Contents

Introduction
Computer Networks

Networking is a strange subject to study – it moves at such a rapid pace that it seems that just as you become familiar with the technology, it becomes outdated and is replaced. If we liken the development of the performance ot the ethernet over the last 10 years to cars, a car that could do 100 mph in 1992 would, in 2002, be doing 10 000 mph. As is usual for computing, the price would also fall dramatically. Working solely on cost, if a car cost £20,000 in 1994, the better equivalent would retail in 2002 for £60.

Networking is the fastest-growing area of computing and it has a huge skills shortage. In late 2001 Cisco (the world's largest networking company) forecast that there would be almost three quarters of a million unfilled networking vacancies across Europe, the Middle East and Africa by the year 2003. Average salaries in networking are also high. In 2002 Cisco reported the average starting salary of a Cisco-certified Network Associate (CCNA) was £30 000, whilst a Cisco-certified Networking Professional (CCNP) was £70,000. (For more information, see *cisco.sunderland.ac.uk*).

Which courses does the book cover?

This book has been designed for students studying general networking and will be useful to any course that covers computer networking. Networking is a huge subject and as a student studying general networking, depth of coverage is neither what you need nor want. Instead, this book provides a solid overview of general networking, explaining the concepts and providing you with enough information to study successfully at least five possible courses:

- EDEXCEL Computer Networking module
- General Degree networking module
- General Foundation Degree networking module
- General Masters degree networking module
- Basic introduction to Computer Networking perhaps as preparation for CCNA courses

This book is intended to provide you with enough theory to aid your understanding and, where possible, with some practical skills – for example, Chapter 7 gives you the basic practical skills to analyse and design small computer networks.

Learning outcomes

Almost all UK courses of study in networking are aligned with the Quality Assurance Agency (QAA) code of practice, which requires learning outcomes to be specified for each module of a programme and the programme overall. This book is aligned with this practice and, at the beginning of each chapter you will find details of the learning outcomes addressed. Overall, the book covers the following learning outcomes:

- To understand network principles, applications and definitions of a computer network, including remote access, email, cost/benefits, intranets, extranets and the Internet.
- To understand networking resources, including facilities provided, hardware, software, security, constraints, performance and licensing.

- To understand and be able to undertake the design and evaluation of computer networks, including the ISO 7 layer model, topologies, communication devices, popular technologies, the TCP/IP model, capacity planning and network design.
- To be able to undertake simple management of computer networks – management of users, groups, workgroups, security implications and responsibilities. Elements of good practice concerning computer viruses, monitoring, estimating resource usage and connection to the outside world.
- To understand the basic principles involved in setting up a computer network including the basic steps of installation and customisation of LINUX and developing login scripts, file systems and file system security.

Using learning outcomes to plan your study

Learning outcomes are intended to be assessed directly, and you must demonstrate competence in them all. Be careful here – if you pass one out of two assignments with 100% and decide to skip the second, you will most probably fail as you haven't demonstrated competence in all learning outcomes. **The bottom line is: don't miss an assessment.**

There are two possible ways you can be assessed: either by an assignment/practical or by a time-constrained test (TCT) or exam. Your assignment comes first, and you can use the content of the assignment to cross off the learning outcomes it covers – in some institutions the learning outcomes covered are printed on the front of the assignment. As there is little point in assessing the same learning outcome twice, you will therefore have a fairly good idea what is going to be covered in the exam/TCT.

Networking has both practical and theoretical elements to it. Most institutions do not have the resources to allow students to set up a computer network or to 'play' with the equipment. As such, practical assessments are likely to be limited to designing a computer network, to producing a user guide on the installation of a networked operating system or to undertaking a capacity planning exercise. The theoretical aspects lend themselves to being covered in the exam/TCT. Chapter 12 provides you with sample practical and theoretical assessments.

What's in the book

In a nutshell, this book covers the basics you would need to know if studying a general computer networking module as part of any further or higher education course of study. If you are studying a specialist course (for example networked computing), you will still find it a useful study guide but will certainly require more depth in certain areas which should be apparent from the lectures you attend.

Tips and tricks

The main tips and tricks associated with studying computer networking are as follows:

- Get used to memorising and drawing diagrams – they help you understand, explain and demonstrate your understanding to the examiner.
- Try to learn a phrase or saying that will help you remember sequences or theories (this book offers a number of suggestions).
- Try to think of an everyday example of the item you are studying (this book offers a number of suggestions).
- Ensure you understand the key parts before you move on.
- Maintain a log book of acronyms and their meaning. Try to commit these to memory (see Glossary).
- Ask when you are unsure.

Textbooks

Rather than specify textbooks for further study at the beginning of the book, I have recommended further reading on a chapter-by-chapter basis. A general tip would be to avoid the large computer networking books if you are only studying the subjects at an introductory level – they are likely to confuse rather than help you.

Good luck in your studies.

Key to symbols used in this book

Organisation network	FDDI concentrator
Ethernet network	Mainframe/mini-computer system
Communications link	ATM cellplex
The Internet	Server
Bridge	Tablet PC
Firewall	PC
Router	Personal digital assistant (PDA)
Switch	Laptop computer
Wireless link	Wireless access point
Multistation access unit (MAU)	Multiplexor
Repeater	Terminal

Symbols courtesy of Cisco networking academy

Chapter 1
Introduction to networks

Chapter summary

This chapter provides an introduction to computer networks and networking. When studying computer networking, it is important to understand that it has evolved and will continue to evolve. As new technologies become available, the uses to which that technology is being put (and *can* be put) will also evolve. A computer network can be categorised according to the geographical area it covers as well as by the type of access it provides to the outside world.

Learning outcomes

After studying this chapter you should aim to test your achievement of the following outcomes. You should be able to:

Outcome 1: Evolution of networks
Understand the way in which computer networks have evolved and the principal stages of this evolution. Question 1 at the end of this chapter will test your ability to do this.

Outcome 2: Two main types of networked computing
Understand the two main categories of computer networking and be able to describe the differences. Question 2 at the end of this chapter will test your ability to do this.

Outcome 3: Network categories
Understand and be able to describe what is meant by the terms LAN, WAN, MAN, PAN, VLAN, VPN, intranet, Internet and extranet. Question 3 at the end of this chapter will test your ability to do this.

How will you be assessed on this?

Assessors want you to demonstrate your knowledge; they don't want you to regurgitate the contents of a book. By understanding networks and their evolution you will be better placed to demonstrate your knowledge. The subject matter of this chapter could be assessed on its own (see the end of chapter questions) or it could be linked with the answer to another question.

CRUCIAL TIP

Diagrams, diagrams, and diagrams! Computer networking is complex and becomes even more complex the more we study it. One of the key ways of picking up marks and of saving time in assessments is to use **diagrams**. A diagram in networking is 'worth a thousand words'. Diagrams aren't particularly difficult to memorise and will impress the assessor with your command of the subject.

Section 1

The evolution of computer networks

Computer networks have been evolving for almost half a century. During this time organisations have become critically dependent upon the services provided by these networks and, today, there are few organisations that could survive without them. This section traces the milestones in the evolution of computer networks.

What are computer networks?

There are many definitions of computer networks but they all have one thing in common: a computer network facilitates the exchange (and processing) of data (and information) between two or more interconnected devices (or points/nodes).

Early computer systems

The earliest computer systems usually comprised a mainframe computer that had little or no interaction with other machines (Figure 1.1). The costs of this equipment were huge and so the time spent working on them had to be maximised to justify the costs involved. However, the processing power of these machines was extremely limited (probably not more than equivalent of today's average digital watch). Programmers produced punched cards or paper tape containing code, whilst data-input clerks produced punch tapes (or paper tape) of the data to be input into the machine. These tapes were then taken to the 'machine room' where the computer was housed, were fed in, processed and the results printed out.

Figure 1.1   Early computer systems
(diagram courtesy of Prof. J. Tait, University of Sunderland)

These early computer systems had enormous benefits for the large organisations that owned them. Routine systems, such as payroll, sales and purchase order processing, were amongst the first systems to be computerised. However, the benefits they brought – although huge – were limited by the manner in which the programs and data had to be fed into the computer, and there was no interactive computing – everything was fed in via punched cards (or paper tape).

The code these earlier programmers used was in a format people could not read. It was put on to punched cards or paper tape and fed into the machine for compilation or execution. Compilation and logic errors were then printed, and the programmers had to work 'off-line' on these error messages, amending the punched cards and often rekeying the batch. Today, editing and recompiling code are done online, as a result of the development of networks. Hence a modern programmer's time is used more efficiently than that of early programmers. It was not long, therefore, before the demand grew for more interaction with the computer.

─── CRUCIAL CONCEPT ───

In early systems, all the equipment was in one room and was controlled totally by the computer operators. There was no connectivity outside the computer room.

Local interactive terminals

As computer systems developed, their processing power increased and they were given secondary storage (tapes, disks). In terms of networks this phase of development was important. Although early computers had a main console, terminals were now attached to computer systems for the first time. Often in the form of a teletype (a combined printer and typewriter), these terminals enabled users to interact with the computer. The terminals were connected directly to the computer but were in the same area of the building as the mainframe computer (Figure 1.2). These links were nearly always made using serial lines (RS232), which meant a limited distance (typically a maximum of 15 m or 45 ft) and limited speed but none the less, they heralded the first computer network. Interactive computing was born and programmers could now edit, compile and execute their code online.

Figure 1.2   Local interactive terminals
(diagram courtesy of Prof. J. Tait, University of Sunderland)

A further important advance occurred in the operating system. Previously, operating systems would typically only support one user and one task (single user, single task). Now the operating system had to support multiple users and multiple tasks (multi-user, multi-tasking). (A full discussion of the types of operating systems can be found in Chapter 8.)

───── CRUCIAL CONCEPT ─────

Local users could now edit and control the running of their own programs.

Remote access

As the concept of interactive computing became more widely known, people in other buildings and at other sites also wanted to gain access to the computers. A method was developed to support this – terminals were connected via modems (modulator/demodulators) and telephone lines (Figure 1.3). These allowed the use of normal dial-up telephone lines as simple (unfortunately, though, slow and unreliable), long-distance computer connections.

Just as they are today, modems were used to connect the terminals and remote computer systems to a telephone line, carrying the data over a line designed to carry voice traffic. Hence, the modem carried out a digital-to-analogue conversion. The speed of these modems was about 300 bits per second (bps), compared with today's typical speeds of 56 000 bps. However, the volume of data transmitted was not as great, as these devices worked only in characters.

Figure 1.3   Remote modem connections
(diagram courtesy of Prof. J. Tait, University of Sunderland)

The telephone lines were provided by telecomms providers (such as BT) and were normal telephone lines in almost every sense – they passed through normal telephone exchanges and could be dialled up. Programmers and users no longer needed to work in the same building as the computer, and so many large organisations used this technology to provide terminals in their local offices. For example, electricity companies provided terminals at their local branches and local authorities installed terminals in their libraries for automated library systems.

CRUCIAL CONCEPT

Users were now able to access the computer system remotely through a telephone line. Organisations were able to use this technology to provide remote access to branch offices.

Leased lines

By the middle to late 1970s many larger organisations had more than one computer and their staff needed regular access to data and computing facilities at sites other than their base. The scale of communication, as well as the required speed and reliability, meant that modem connection through the ordinary, switched telephone network could no longer support their needs. This led to the adoption of permanently connected long-distance lines between two end points terminating in an organisation's own premises (usually provided by telephone companies). Such lines could span the country or even the world. These connections are known as **leased lines** (Figure 1.4) and are still offered by most communication service providers today although, in practice, they rarely offer the fixed wire copper connection of years gone by. Leased line networks were the first real wide area networks and were the forerunners of packet switched networks and such modern developments as Asynchronous Transfer Mode (ATM) networks.

Leased lines were analogue and, as such, still required modems. However, the modems used were high quality and high speed, delivering up to 14 400 bps. The links were secure and costs were based on line rental rather than call costs. Usually, their capacity was far in excess of the capacity needed by a single terminal and, to utilise the line to its fullest, multiplexors were developed and added to either end of the link. The purpose of a multiplexor is to share the line capacity amongst a number of terminals. In Figure 1.5 there are two terminals connected to the multiplexor. As the multiplexor is a simple Time Division Multiplexor (TDM) it will share the time slot (e.g. 1 second) between the two terminals in short bursts. Therefore each terminal will get half the time slot, in this instance, half a second each. The multiplexors at each end of the line are synchronised with each other, which will ensure that the correct data is passed down the correct serial line. In practice, eight terminals would be typically linked through a multiplexor. This arrangement was common up until the mid-1990s.

Figure 1.4   Leased line networks
(diagram courtesy of Prof. J. Tait, University of Sunderland)

Leased lines continued to extend the benefits networks were offering organisations. Heralding the first, real, Wide Area Network (WAN), they allowed more access from remote locations (such as local offices) through the sharing of a private line. Utility companies and local authorities deployed such systems to give local offices access to the centrally held information. It is important to note, however, that such access cannot be considered client/ server (see section 2) as the users are using dumb terminals (terminals with no computing power) – simply a monitor and a keyboard.

Figure 1.5   Leased line arrangement using multiplexors

── CRUCIAL CONCEPT──

Leased lines provided remote users with high-security, high-speed dedicated links, which increased the opportunities for remote access to the computer system.

Local area networks

By the late 1970s many organisations (large and small) had more than one computer. This trend accelerated rapidly in the early 1980s with the availability of powerful (for that time) standalone personal computers (PCs) – a trend that continues to the present day. The method of access at this time meant that users needed one terminal per system, but demand grew for PCs to be able to access many systems (including other PCs) and to transfer files. This led to the need for a system that was capable of transferring data at high speed between different sorts of computers typically located close together at the same site or in the same building.

This need was answered by the development of modern high-speed local area networks (LANs), such as the ethernet and token ring. The mid-1980s saw the introduction of these in many organisations, but they came into even more widespread use in the 1990s. These technologies bridge the gap between high-speed computer-room networks (parallel interfaces, etc.) and low-speed serial interfaces (e.g. RS-232) (see the earlier section 'Local interactive terminals'). They allowed multiple devices to be connected via a shared transmission medium (Figure 1.6). Since their inception, a number of LAN technologies have been developed and, in the early days, there were a number of standards for LANs, including Arcnet (for the BBC micros) and the Cambridge ring. As often happens, the market has largely settled on a few technologies, primarily the ethernet but also the token ring (these will be discussed in detail in Chapters 3 and 5). LANs further extended the benefits networks offer by allowing the interconnection of multiple computing facilities (such as PCs, mainframes and mini-computers) through a high-speed link.

Figure 1.6   Local area networks (diagram courtesy of Prof. J. Tait, Unversity of Sunderland)

CRUCIAL CONCEPT

LANs provided easy-to-establish, high-speed connectivity between any connected devices but with limited distances.

Quick test

Briefly outline the major stages in the evolution of networks.

Types of networked computing

The main purpose of computer networking is to provide an organisation with services. Initially, this was for interactive computing but, with the introduction of PCs, the network has evolved to allow communication between PCs and also to provide services such as shared printing, shared disk access, etc. Networks typically provide these services to a client from either a dedicated server (known as client/server computing or networking) or from a peer computer (known as peer-to-peer networking). Networks constructed with a server are often said to have a client/server architecture, and those with a community of equals are often said to have a peer-to-peer architecture. Understanding these architectures is fundamental to the study of networking.

Introduction

All networked computing facilities can be grouped into two architectures:

- peer-to-peer networking;
- client/server networking.

Both architectures are intended for different uses and require networked operating systems (NOS) to support them.

CRUCIAL CONCEPT

The fundamental difference between the two architectures is that client/server architectures require a dedicated server whereas, with peer-to-peer networks, there is no separate server and the work of the server is shared between the connected computers. Comparing Figures. 1.7 and 1.8 (see below) you will notice that Figure 1.8 does not have a server. However, the physical connections to the media are still the same.

Client/server computing

This is the traditional model of networked computing (Figure 1.7). Here clients make requests of a server (the diagrams shows a single-server system) and the server then carries out the request and provides a response to the client. This model has been in operation for many years and we have all probably encountered it at some point. It is 'full blown' networking architecture and is supported by all network operating system vendors, such as Novell and even Microsoft in Windows NT and 2000. It is also supported by all versions of UNIX.

Figure 1.7   Typical client/server architecture

Key to this architecture is that there is (at least) one serving computer (the server) which provides all the client machines with the facilities they need – usually file and printer sharing. Although these services might seem trivial, they revolutionised computing. Without a network, sharing files was a real problem requiring users to share a floppy disk. As can be imagined, many problems arise from sharing a floppy disk, the most obvious being, of course, the inconvenience of having physically to take the disk to the other user. Others include the compatibility and reliability of floppy disks and their limited capacity. In some cases, sharing a floppy disk is impossible – consider a gig or cinema booking system with multiple users trying to access the same file: could they really operate by sharing a floppy disk?

Specialist printers (such as colour laser printers) can be expensive and might not be used very often. By attaching such devices to a server, their facilities are made available to all network users, giving everyone access with minimal inconvenience.

As the client/server architecture and its supporting Network Operating Systems (commonly called a NOS) have developed, other facilities have been added. For example, users can now be allocated to groups and security can be increased through the allocation of rights to those groups who need access to specific files or devices. Files can also be accessed simultaneously by many users (although locking controls need to be in place to stop two users updating the same record at the same time). Printers have queues , which allows a client machine to send its entire print job to the server for processing – thus freeing up the client machine's own processing capacity. Some NOSs work on different types of computers allowing the machines to 'talk' to each other. An example of this is Novell Netware, which is available for Mac and PC platforms. Email facilities also require a central server.

Client/server computing has undoubtedly revolutionised computing and provides benefits almost all organisations desire. The advantages far outweigh the disadvantages. The principal disadvantage, however, is cost – with client/server computing, there is a need to purchase a central serving machine that should be fast and have huge storage capacity. Such machines are not cheap and this sometimes puts them out of the reach of smaller businesses – enter the alternative approach of peer-to-peer networking!

One other disadvantage to client/server computing is the reliance upon one central system for the provision of services. If something happens to that machine, access to all the information and to the services of that machine is lost. Therefore competent personnel are required to manage client/server architectures.

CRUCIAL CONCEPT

With client/server network architectures, there is (at least one) server that is a dedicated machine providing services to the client. This machine may be unusable other than through one of its client computers.

Peer-to-peer networking

Peer-to-peer networking is a low-cost way of providing some of the more popular benefits of networks at a fraction of the cost of a full-blown NOS. Its major benefit is, again, the sharing of resources printers, files, faxes, etc. The fundamental difference between client/server and peer-to-peer computing, however, is that with peer-to-peer networks, **there is no central server** (Figure 1.8). The tasks a server would normally perform are shared between the client machines themselves. For example, a shared printer would be connected to a client machine rather than being connected to the server. Similarly, data to be shared would reside on a client machine rather than on the server. Often all that is needed to establish a peer-to-peer network is the network cabling itself and a version of an operating system that supports peer-to-peer networking (e.g. Windows 3.11, 95, 98, 2000, XP, etc.).

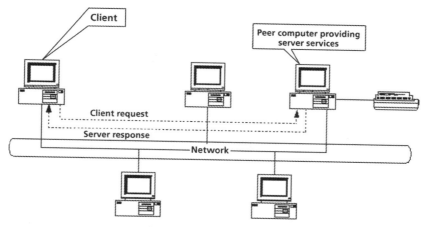

Figure 1.8 Typical peer-to-peer network

Peer-to-peer networks obtain their name from the fact that, while each machine is being used by a user (a client), it may also be serving another computer (therefore acting as a server). Thus the conventional terms 'client' or 'server' are not applicable as, in this network, the machines are a community of 'equals' (peers). As there is no requirement for an expensive server and the machines usually have the appropriate software installed, peer-to-peer networking is a low-cost solution for smaller businesses or isolated pockets in large organisations. Because this type of networking is often found in small offices, it is sometimes referred to as 'small office computing'.

Whilst it is possible to have a peer-to-peer network of large servers (for example, UNIX servers), this is not generally what is meant by the definition of peer-to-peer networking and certainly not what is meant here. Peer-to-peer networking is really only suitable for small installations. Microsoft recommend a maximum of ten computers. After this, not only will throughput deteriorate but also the general performance of the machines. It is not possible to give an exact figure because it depends upon how the computers are being used – if lots of disk and file sharing is going on, performance issues may arise with only four computers. Conversely, if there is little sharing of devices, both the network and the computers might operate satisfactorily with up to ten or more machines.

CRUCIAL TIP

Microsoft recommends a maximum of ten machines in a peer-to-peer network.

The vendors of peer-to-peer network operating systems have made their set-up very simple, thus avoiding the need for specialist network management skills. Overall, peer-to-peer networks are most useful to smaller organisations who wish to try out networking in a small way or to larger organisations wishing to solve small problems. Usually there is little or no planning, and such environments are usually fairly stable in terms of the user base, and are only used for sharing a few resources. Examples would be a Managing Director and a Personal Assistant (PA) in a large organisation who link their machines to transfer data (files, letters, reports, etc.) and small office computing (e.g. a small law firm or a small estate agent who require file and printer sharing). Whilst isolated pockets in large organisations are not recommended, peer-to-peer networking can sometimes help provide limited connectivity as a stop-gap measure until the IT department is are able to connect all the users. Small businesses, on the other hand, can use peer-to-peer networking whilst they expand and grow. The relatively low start-up costs, however, must be weighed against the possibilities for limited expansion, although investment in a company's peer-to-peer technology would not necessarily be lost when it was big enough to expand into a full client/server situation.

Peer-to-peer networking has many advantages for the small organisation, but it also has its disadvantages. In a client/server network, the server is a powerful machine, reflecting the amount of work it does. If a peer-to-peer network is installed instead, the processing normally associated with a server has to be undertaken by the client machines themselves. This means that, as well as processing the task in hand, the machine must also undertake additional processing at someone else's request. Ultimately, this results in an overall degeneration in the machine's performance.

Security is also an issue. Whilst peer-to-peer NOS manufacturers have made setting up these networks relatively easy, they have placed security in the hands of inexperienced users who might mostly be unaware of the consequences of their actions. Therefore, there are often glaring security gaps in such installations.

The random distribution of resources can be a further problem with peer-to-peer networking. If the data is shared among many machines and one fails or cannot be started, it can be difficult to predict the consequences of such failure. For example, peer-to-peer networking often won't begin until a certain user has logged into his or her computer. Imagine a situation in a small business where someone powers off his or her PC on a Friday evening before going on holiday for two weeks. If that machine cannot be started without the password, no one in the organisation can access the data on it. If the data is payroll information, no one might be paid until the user returns from holiday. For security reasons, however, the password should not be shared.

CRUCIAL CONCEPT

With peer-to-peer networking it is the method of accessing resources that differs from client/server networking. In peer-to-peer networking, there is no server, and access to files, printers and other resources is provided by the user machines.

Summary

Both client/server and peer-to-peer networking have their advantages and disadvantages and careful consideration should be given to these when choosing the correct one for an organisation. It is always best to choose a client/server architecture unless there are compelling reasons for choosing a peer-to-peer network. It is also important to note that both architectures need a network technology (cables, cards, etc.) to operate on (technologies are covered in Chapter 3).

Quick test

Briefly list the differences between client/server and peer-to-peer network architectures.

Section 3

Network categories

Networks can be classified into three distinct types, although the boundaries between these types are somewhat blurred. This section reviews the different categories of network and identifies the key differences between them.

Introduction

Networks are often classified into three types depending upon the geographical area they cover and according to some other distinguishing factors. It is necessary to understand the differences between them in terms of performance, geographic coverage, limitations of connection speed and degree of choice in the service provided, etc. The three common categories are:

- Local Area Networks (LANs);
- Metropolitan Area Networks (MANs);
- Wide Area Networks (WANs)

although a new category is emerging – Personal Area Networks (PANs) – as well as new terms – Virtual Local Area Networks (VLANs) and Virtual Private Networks (VPNs).

Local area network (LAN)

Local area networks (or LANs, as they are called) cover, with the exception of PANs, the smallest geographical area for networks. Despite this, they are the most popular category, and LANs often have hundreds if not thousands of connections. LANs, as their name suggests, are intended to be local and small, although now this is not necessarily the case. When this type of network was first devised, a typical LAN would have been a classroom, an office or, at most, a few offices. Now LANs cover entire floors or even entire buildings and with buildings such as universities, colleges and call centres that is a lot of connections!

LANs usually offer the highest speed of all network types as the media used in such networks are controlled by the organisations themselves and so, any constraints on the implementation of the technology are the responsibility of the organisations using them. For example, a organisation in the middle of the countryside is free to implement whatever media it desires for its LAN: it simply needs to buy the necessary equipment and install it. It could also have whatever speed LAN current technology supports. Should it wish to connect to a telecommunications provider (e.g. BT), the speed of connection would then be limited to what the provider can offer, which, in some parts of the countryside, is likely to be limited.

CRUCIAL CONCEPT

The characteristics of a LAN are as follows:
It is usually based in one building.
The speed of the technology is at the organisation's discretion.
The management and maintenance of the network are the organisation's responsibility.
There is a choice of technology.
There is no outside involvement from telecommunications providers.

Metropolitan area networks (MANs)

MANs are larger than LANs yet they are contained within a defined geographical area. A good example of a MAN is a university campus where several buildings are connected together across a city or town or several universities or colleges are connected across a region. The media used in a MAN may be the jurisdiction of the organisation itself or may belong to one or more telecomms providers (in which case the speed may be restricted). The real determining factor in who provides the media, however, is cost. Although UK law currently allows for any organisation to lay its own cables, the cost of doing so safely and without risk to the public is high. The longer the cable run, the more expensive this becomes, and so it is often cheaper to contract with a telecomms provider who can provide the link at a lower cost.

MANs frequently don't belong to a single organisation but are a city or regional resource. An example of this is the NORthern Metropolitan Area Network (NORMAN), which is a network in the North East of England linking together the universities in the area and providing them with a very high-speed Internet connection. Because they use the services of a telecomms provider, MANs usually run at a slower speed than a LAN. However, they span a larger geographic area than a LAN and are either managed/maintained by both the organisation and the telecomms provider or are the sole responsibility of the organisation.

CRUCIAL CONCEPT

MANs cover the ground somewhere between LANs and WANs (see the next section). They can be contained within an organisation's site or they may be a regional resource. They generally operate on lines leased from a communications provider and, hence, they operate at a lower speed than a LAN.

Wide area networks (WANs)

WANs cover a geographical area beyond that of a MAN – perhaps all an organisation's offices in a country or even beyond national boundaries (a good example would be a multinational organisation with offices in different countries). WANs are almost always dependent upon telecomms providers, as the length of the media runs is huge and prohibitively expensive.

As WANs are dependent upon telecomms providers, the speed of the link is likely to be limited compared with a MAN or a LAN. For example, the fastest available link (in early 2003) on a LAN is 1 Gbps or 1000 Mbps, and the cost of the equipment to set up a two-station network would be around £2200 (at early 2003 prices). In contrast, the current fastest link on a WAN is 155 Mbps and costs about £155 000 per annum to lease (at early 2003 prices). Until 1998 the fastest link available externally was only about 2 Mbps, and this speed (or slower) could be encountered in many parts of the world where a WAN may have to have made a link. Maintenance of the WAN is shared between the organisation and the telecomms provider. When selecting a WAN link it is important to ensure that the provider will correct any faults in a timely manner – especially if the organisation is critically dependent upon the link.

CRUCIAL TIP

Just as a chain is only as strong as its weakest link, so the speed of a network is usually only as fast as its slowest link.

CRUCIAL CONCEPT

WANS are differentiated in the following ways:
By the large geographic area they cover.
They almost always use a telecomms provider.
They are slower than a MAN or LAN link.
They possibly depend upon a number of telecomms providers (if they are international networks.
Maintenance is shared between the telecomms provider and the organisation.

Personal area networks (PANs)

PANs are very new and are intended to link personal computing devices (such as organisers, mobile phones and laptops) within a personal area – an area of around 2 m. Although only just emerging, it is the intention that PANs will do away with wires. Each of the devices in a PAN would be fitted with a radio communications card (working in Ghz), which will allow it to communicate with several other devices simultaneously. One of the better known PAN technologies is Bluetooth. Bluetooth is a consortium of manufacturers who are working to ensure its specification will allow worldwide connection (more information can be found at *www.bluetooth.com*). As the number of personal computing devices continues to grow and pressure mounts to make them communicate, this is sure to be an expanding area.

─────── CRUCIAL TIP ───────

One of the most common mistakes made by students is to forget that networks are measured in megabits per second (Mbps) and that data is measured in megabytes (MB). There are 8 bits in a byte and failure to work in bits rather than bytes puts you out by a factor of 8. Thus 1 MB of data to be transferred is 8 Mb.

Virtual local area networks (VLANs)

Often, an organisation wishes to subdivide its LAN – for example, the accounts or personnel department may wish to keep its network secure whilst still being connected to the organisational LAN. This can be achieved using VLANs. VLAN technology is a by-product of switching technology (see Chapter 6), allowing a LAN to be subdivided into several virtual LANs. There is no difference in the physical structure of the LAN but the switches deployed are configured to segregate traffic. Figure 1.9 shows a typical VLAN configuration. Here the network is divided into three separate VLANs. As with a normal LAN, the data passes through the organisation backbone but, this time, it is tagged, identifying the VLAN to which it belongs. Data is only distributed within the VLAN, which provides greater security.

VLANs can be configured in one of two ways:

- Making the switch port a member of the VLAN. Thus any computer plugged into the port will become a member of that VLAN. This is known as a port centric.
- Via the MAC address (see Chapter 3). Each machine has a unique address (called the MAC address). This can be used to determine VLAN membership. Thus VLAN membership is determined by the computer's MAC address, irrespective of the port to which it is connected. This is more secure than port centric as a potential hacker would need to gain access to a computer which is a member of the VLAN. This type of configuration is known as dynamic.

Figure 1.9   Network divided into VLANs

CRUCIAL TIP

Not all switches support VLANs.

Intranets/Internet

Networks are also classified according to their connection to the 'general public'. Categorised as intranets, the Internet and extranets, this classification can be used to determine whether access to the network is from a closed group or from all groups.

Intranet

Intranets are networks that provide the facilities we have come to expect from the World Wide Web, such as web pages, file transfer, form filling, etc., but they provide these to a closed group only, normally controlled by a password. For example, the XYZ Widget company may have several sales executives travelling and meeting with customers. As support for these executives, the company wants them to have access to production schedules, customer information and costing details. If they had been based in the company offices the network would provide them with this information. As the information will constantly change, it isn't feasible continuously to send them disks containing the information. Using the Internet would solve the problem but the data is sensitive. The dilemma here is that they need the facilities of the network but they need them outside the building, and the Internet can provide these but the information is confidential.

This is an ideal candidate for an intranet –the executives can go to the company's website and then select the private area (or a more secure method is to have a separate URL that isn't advertised). The executives are authenticated in some way and then allowed access to the sensitive data contained in the site.

The name 'Intranet' is sometimes used to describe an 'internal' internet based upon files that are only open to users of the company's LAN. Although this is not exactly what is meant by the term intranet – because it is providing web facilities to a closed group – it can be regarded as an intranet.

Virtual private networks (VPNs)

Whilst the facilities intranets provide are extremely useful, there is a potential security risk in that the data can be 'eavesdropped' as it travels across the Internet. VPNs offer a solution to this by encrypting the data before it travels across the Internet. VPNs are set up by configuring the roaming machine as a VPN client, and a machine in the organisation as a VPN server (specialist hardware is available to act as a VPN server, but this task can also be undertaken by a Windows 2000 server or a third party package).

Once configured, the roaming machine can contact the VPN server through the Internet in a conventional manner. Once connected, the VPN server and client go into a predetermined encryption mode and the data is sent between the two in an encrypted format. Once received by the VPN server, the data is decrypted and passed on to the organisational LAN (Figure 1.10). At this point, the data from the roaming machine assumes the identity of the VPN server, giving it access to the organisational LAN.

When sent back to the roaming client, the data passes through the VPN server where it is encrypted before being passed on to the Internet. Upon receipt, the client decrypts the data for presentation to the user. This is a standard feature of Windows from 2000 onwards and can be found in Network Connections (see Windows Help).

Figure 1.10   Roaming machine contacting the organisational LAN through a VPN

Internet

The word 'Internet' is an abbreviation of internetwork – literally meaning a 'network of interconnected networks' – a definition that can be applied to many networks which could be part of the Internet or independent of it. Thus the Internet we all know (i.e. carrying web traffic) is effectively a worldwide internetwork of networks.

An example of an internetwork is a college or university that has a large number of network connections. Just as with a road, the more users who use it, the more congested it becomes and the slower everything runs. To ease such problems, the number of machines connected to a network is restricted and divided up into several, smaller networks. To provide the same functionality, the networks have to be 'internetworked' together, thus forming an Internet. In a large college or university, this internetwork is likely to comprise many smaller networks and can itself be connected to the Internet.

The Internet itself, when conceived, was a network of networks. Designed by the Advanced Research Projects Agency (ARPA) of the US Department of Defense (DoD) in the 1960s, the Internet was developed to span military bases across the world and to connect their networks. It needed to be robust and to be able to operate in the event of a nuclear strike. It was later extended to those organisations that worked with the DoD – for example universities and suppliers. As the Internet became more widely known, more and more institutions wanted to be connected (especially academic institutions) and the number of connections on the Internet rose.

Until the early to mid-1990s, the Internet mainly carried text-based traffic (such as emails and files), although the standards for file transfer and remote login, etc. already existed. Any search was performed by a text-based utility called a gopher. In the early 1990s, CERN introduced a hypertext system allowing text to be linked over the Internet (just as Microsoft Help files are linked). By 1994, the National Center for Supercomputer Applications (NCSA) enhanced this with its Mosaic browser, providing a graphical user interface (GUI) hypertext-based system. As anyone who has created a web page will know, the majority of a basic web page is text. Some elements are enclosed in tags (e.g. <P>), which are recognised by the browser and displayed in a particular way. This revolutionised the Internet and created the World Wide Web (www) which everyone wants to be a part of. However, the Internet is still the carrier of the web!

Extranets

Extranets are a popular discussion topic at the moment. An extranet essentially means extending access to an institution's network to its suppliers. Extranets are very popular because they can bring huge benefits. For example, a car manufacturer could extend access to its production network to its synchronous suppliers. By using this access, the suppliers could determine what cars were to be made that week and could ensure that they manufactured the correct components (for example, seats) to go into the cars. Obviously, the seats would need to be the correct model and colour. In turn, by making their production schedule available to their own suppliers, the suppliers can ensure that the correct fabric is produced. In this example, none of the companies would need to hold much stock of finished goods but they can still fulfil the orders. By not holding stock they reduce storage and overall operating costs – hence the popularity of extranets.

CRUCIAL CONCEPT

An Internet is a network of networks. The Internet is a publicly accessible information resource. An intranet is essentially an internet for use only within an organisation. An extranet is effectively an intranet that is typically shared among an organisation's suppliers.

Quick test

Identify the major differences between the three categories of networks.

Section 4

End of chapter assessment

Questions

1. Outline the major developments that led to today's networks.
2. Explain the differences and similarities between peer-to-peer and client server networks.
3. Explain what is meant by the terms LAN, MAN and WAN.

Answers

1. To answer this question, you need to review the development of networks from the early days, when computers had no real networks (single-stream systems) up to the introduction of local area networks. In your answer you should include local interactive terminals and remote access through both modem and leased lines. Remember that diagrams are important. If you can draw a diagram it makes your answer easier to mark (always a good ploy), and it shows the assessor you understand. The diagrams are relatively simple and drawing them serves as a prompt for you. At each stage you should also discuss the reasons why networking developed and the benefits each particular phase gave to the users of the network. Ideally you should also discuss any weaknesses of the stage and relate these to the next stage of development to give a smooth flow.

2. As you progress through higher education the aim is to make you a reflective practitioner - someone who can review an idea or a concept critically. The earlier you learn this technique the better – it will allow you to pick up additional marks at Level 1 (HNC and Fd Level 1) and Level 2 (HND and Fd Level 2) because it is not expected there; instead, assessors expect descriptions or explanations – you can go one better! In answering this question you need to provide the assessor with a discussion of both the client/server network architecture and of the peer-to-peer network architecture. If you begin with the discussion of client/server architecture, you can highlight its composition, the benefits it has brought to organisations and any limiting factors (the major one being cost, of course). This will lead you smoothly into a discussion of peer-to-peer networks since these are meant to provide similar benefits to organisations but at less cost.

Again diagrams may help illustrate your answer and will impress the assessor with your command of the subject. Diagrams allow assessors to see at a glance what the physical difference is between peer-to-peer and client/server networking. Extra marks will come from discussing limitations or problems with the architectures – for example, that Microsoft recommend no more than ten computers in a peer-to-peer network. Concluding the answer by discussing which network architecture is appropriate for an example organisation will demonstrate an understanding of the implementation of the subject and gain extra marks.

3. Again, an explanation and, again, diagrams can help with the explanation. The assessor wants you to demonstrate that you know of and understand the three major categories of networking:

- LANs
- MANs
- WANs.

This is your chance to impress with the currency of your knowledge by illustrating that you also know of an emerging category called PANs. Don't spend too much time on PANs as the assessor may have a marking scheme based only on the three, but quote a website or a technology (e.g. Bluetooth) that illustrates your point. A successful answer would list the three categories and then discuss the properties of each of the categories – the geographic area they cover, speed, costs, who administers, any involvement from telecomms providers, etc. Typical applications and uses of the category will help demonstrate you have the ability to apply the knowledge. Don't be afraid to quote a university or college campus, classroom or national/multinational company in the categories, as these are perfect textbook examples.

Section 5

Further reading and research

See the _www.PhilipIrving.com_ website for up-to-date further reading and support for this chapter.

Cisco Networking Academy Program (2001) _First Year Companion Guide_ (2nd edn). Cisco Press. ISBN: 1 58713 025 4. Chapters 1 and 4.

Cisco Networking Academy Program (2001) _Second Year Companion Guide_ (2nd edn). Cisco Press. ISBN: 1 58713 029 7. Chapter 3.

Hodson, P. (2002) _Local Area Networks_ (4th edn). Continuum. ISBN: 0 82645 866 1. Chapter 1.

www.bluetooth.com (accessed 11/4/02).

Chapter 2
The networked system

Chapter summary

Networked computer systems are part of almost every organisation in the western world. And not without good reason: networked computer systems allow organisations unparalleled access to their information irrespective of its geographic location. They make communicating between different machine types possible and, when coupled with the Internet, make ecommerce possible.

Organisations are constantly looking for ways in which they can save money or gain a competitive advantage – networks offer the promise of both.

Learning outcomes

After studying this chapter you should aim to test your achievement of the following outcomes. You should be able to:

Outcome 1: Networked resources
Understand the essential components of any networked system and be able to identify these components. Question 1 at the end of this chapter will test your ability to do this.

Outcome 2: Facilities of a networked operating system
Understand the facilities and benefits a networked operating system (NOS) can provide to an organisation. Question 2 at the end of this chapter will test your ability to do this.

Outcome 3: Capacity issues
Understand that a network has limited bandwidth (capacity) and that applications which run upon the network need to be both suitable and within the capacity of the network. Question 3 at the end of this chapter will test your ability to do this.

Outcome 4: Security implications
Understand that connecting a computer to a network will greatly increase the security risks and be aware of such risks. Question 4 at the end of this chapter will test your ability to do this.

Outcome 5: Licensing issues
Understand the licensing issues associated with networked software and be able to provide advice. Question 5 at the end of this chapter will test your ability to do this.

How will you be assessed on this?

This chapter is very much introductory – setting out the major components of networking and identifying the benefits and issues associated with their use. The ideal assessment in this case would be a case study of an organisation that wished to install a network. A case study would allow you to discuss all you have learnt from this chapter in a manner relevant to the organisation. It is therefore likely that such an assessment will be an assignment. The questions at the end of this chapter form such a case study.

Section 1

Networked resources

Computer networks are essential to most organisations and critical to a high number – that is to say, if the organisation was deprived of its network it would no longer be able to carry out its mission. Such networks are considered 'mission critical'.

It might be thought that such mission critical networks would be restricted to large organisations, but this is not the case. A reasonably large taxi company whose bookings are stored on a computer system and dispatched by that system would consider its network as mission critical. If it was unable to access the server, it would be unable to dispatch the taxis; if it couldn't do that, it couldn't carry out its mission.

There are essential components to any networked system and this section explores these critical components.

Overview of network resources

From Chapter 1 we know that a network provides a means by which two or more computers can communicate. It is desirable to have such communications as they allow the efficient sharing of files and printers and make possible such communications as the web and email. In short, they tie together data, communications, computing and file servers. They also provide a mechanism by which data can be transferred between differing machine types – for example, Apple MACs and PCs.

When considering resources, the best starting point is the computer itself: somehow the computer needs to be enabled to use the network. This is achieved by the installation of a Network Interface Card (or NIC). An NIC interfaces the computer's architecture with that of the network and facilitates connection between the two. Because of this, the NIC is said to be both network media dependent and computer hardware dependent. In short, the NIC you select needs to match both the internal architecture of the computer (e.g. PCI, ESIA, ISA) and the technology/media of the LAN (e.g. 100BaseT ethernet). Figure 2.1 shows a selection of NICs, whilst Figure 2.2 shows the installation of an NIC. All computers which are to communicate over the network need to have NICs installed.

Figure 2.1   A selection of network interface cards (NICs)

Figure 2.2 The installation of a NIC

CRUCIAL CONCEPT

The NIC must match the computer architecture, LAN technology and media. For example a 100BaseT PCI Ethernet card is meant for computers with a PCI slot – Ethernet technology runs over UTP cabling (see Chapters 3 and 5).

The computer is now electrically able to transfer data outside itself but doesn't have any form of connection with other computers and requires communications media. Most commonly, copper cables interconnect the machines. However, there is a variety of other media that are used in computer networking to carry the data – for example, fibre optic is used to carry light, and even air itself is used to carry radio waves (wireless LANs, Bluetooth) and light (infrared communication). To keep things simple we will look at a common medium – copper. Figure 2.3 shows Unshielded Twisted Pair (UTP) cabling which is the most common form of connection today (terminating in an RJ-45 plug).

Figure 2.3   The correctly made-up end of UTP cabling

The media need to be connected to the computers that are being networked, which may require the use of networking devices such as a hub or switch (Figure 2.4) (for further information, see Chapter 5). Our computers are then able to communicate with the outside world and are physically connected together. The final requirement is the software itself! On a Microsoft Windows platform, two pieces of software are necessary:

- driver software for the NIC;
- Windows itself.

Figure 2.4   Computers networked using an ethernet switch

As with most accessories purchased for a PC, NICs are shipped with a driver disk. The driver disk simply allows the computer to use (or 'drive') the hardware and needs to be installed before attempting to network the computer – otherwise the operating system won't be able to find the NIC! Since Windows for workgroups was launched in the mid-1990s the Windows operating system has had the ability to communicate over networks. The network settings can be found in the Control Panel (see Figure 2.5).

Figure 2.5   Control Panel settings; note the networking icon

---

CRUCIAL CONCEPT

Networking requires hardware, software and media. The hardware provides the electrical connection from the computer to the outside world, whilst the media connects the computers together. Networking 'kit' may be used to join the media. The software uses this connection to carry bits of data. This data could be used to share or move anything that is digital.

Quick test

List the essential components of a networked operating system and briefly outline their purpose.

Section 2

Facilities of a networked operating system

Quite simply, networked operating systems (or NOSs) enable almost any make of computer to communicate with almost any other make of computer. Although this sounds relatively simple, it is not – and the power such simple communication provides to an organisation is tremendous. As things continue to 'become digital', digital representation can be effectively moved on a computer network. Thus, as the digital revolution continues, the products can be shipped by the network – making things possible that were never dreamt of.

Why are computer networks so popular?

Networking has, throughout its history, brought huge benefits to organisations. For example, the ability of early programmers to work online was immeasurable in terms of efficiency and effectiveness. Before the advent of PCs in the 1980s, computing was undertaken on either mini or mainframe computers. As these were hugely expensive, organisations with such machines needed to ensure maximum use was being made of them whilst the machines themselves were kept secure. The most effective way of achieving this was via remote access through the network. Thus, in local authorities and large companies throughout the world, the resources of the computer – processing power, disk storage, printing, etc. – were shared, providing maximum benefits for the cost.

In the early 1980s IBM introduced the first PC, which was an instant success with organisations the world over. Processing power was brought to the desktop, as were files and printing devices. Having the files and printers local to a machine was, at first, a novelty – users were in charge of their own data, printing and processing power. Organisations very quickly realised that, although there were benefits to this approach, there were also drawbacks. Files, which needed to be shared, had to be swapped physically (sometimes referred to as 'sneakernet' – which comes from walking around with a disk); expensive printing resources had to be duplicated; and the organisation's data was decentralised and difficult to access. Take, for example, the booking office taking bookings for a popular gig we looked at briefly in Chapter 1. The seating area (file) needs to be shared amongst everyone taking the bookings, otherwise over- or under-booking may occur. This cannot be effectively undertaken by sharing a floppy disk! As this example illustrates, the sharing of information in an organisation is critical. To most organisations, communication and the sharing of information are critical. A sales department may ask: 'Can production handle this extra order if we take it?' If production keep their data local, this will be difficult to find out and the order might be lost.

LANs were soon added to the PC platform providing a means where the users could have their processing power locally but could share information and other resources such as expensive printers. The first LANs introduced to the PC environment were client/server LANs and, today, the majority still are. However, such are the benefits provided by LANs that smaller organisations have introduced peer-to-peer LANs to provide similar benefits. As

LANs have evolved, so have the benefits they provide. Early LANs provided facilities for file and printer sharing. Today, LANs provide many more benefits to the organisation. For example:

- They can facilitate distributed processing (where the server can process, for example, a database query before returning the results to the client).
- Email facilities and file transfer.
- Remote backup.
- Video conferencing.
- Fax.
- Shared applications, such as accounting and payroll systems (subject to licence terms).
- Shared data.

Using email as an example, few would argue that email has revolutionised communication. For example, in 1992, a fire at a chemical plant sent a toxic cloud over the north east. The university in which I work had one call from the police advising everyone to stay inside. Relaying this life-threatening information to 1500 employees was achieved in seconds using email. Staff could then inform students to stay inside.

Sharing information (such as working documents) with colleagues is difficult and time-consuming without email (the file would have to be copied to one disk per colleague and put in the internal post). It is much more effective to use email and simply attach the file. The network, therefore, also has to provide the translation between different machine types. Thus a Mac computer can send and receive emails from a PC which is easier than sharing floppy disks (due to the different formats between MACs and PCs) . The phrase 'information is power' is certainly true. The organisation that can share and access the information the quickest is likely to be the one that progresses the fastest. In every sense, networks provide an organisation with many ways of communicating more effectively. The fact that the cost of providing these facilities is relatively low means that the networks are providing low-cost/high-benefit solutions to an organisation – hence their popularity and continued growth.

CRUCIAL CONCEPT

Networking has brought many benefits to organisations, allowing them to realise huge savings. Such a positive cost-benefit has fuelled the development of networks. Organisations can almost always benefit from enhancing their networks.

Quick test

Identify the benefits networks bring to an organisation and, hence, why they are so popular.

Section 3

Capacity and performance issues

Computer networks bring enormous benefits to an organisation and, therefore, organisations often become critically dependent upon their networks. Unfortunately, computer networks do not have unlimited capacity, and it is important to realise that this can often be a limiting factor. This is particularly so when connecting externally, either via a WAN or the Internet. (Chapter 7 covers capacity in more detail.)

Capacity limitations

Perhaps the single most limiting factor of a computer network is its capacity to carry data. Unfortunately, networks lag behind computer architectures in terms of the amount of information they can pass from point to point. This is due, in part, to networks providing serial as opposed to parallel transmission. It is also due to the fact that the network is shared amongst many computers, where the faster internal architecture of a computer is reserved for its own use.

It is often helpful to think of a computer network in terms of plumbing. No one would dream of supplying the water needs to a twenty-storey hotel from a garden hose! There obviously isn't enough capacity in a garden hose – it isn't big enough to let the required amount of water through and neither is the tap. If such a water supply was used, the water would slow to a trickle for each user, and the problem would become more acute during peak times – early morning and when many people wanted a bath (high-volume users). In fact, if the water was fed from the bottom of the building it is likely that, during peak times, only the bottom floor would have a supply. This is because there is insufficient capacity. We can substitute the hotel for a computer LAN (say, 30 stations) and the garden hose for the LAN technology. If we have 10Base2 (see Chapter 5), we have a maximum of 7 Mbps (technically 10Base2 has a theoretical maximum of 10 Mbps but in practice it's nearer 7 Mbps) shared amongst every user of the LAN. Thus in every second we can transfer a maximum of 7 Mbps for all computers. To take an example, poor-quality video is approximately 10 MB per minute: 10 MB $\times$ 8 = 80 Mbits. This tells us that each machine requires 1.34 Mbps capacity to show the video over a LAN. If we have 30 machines, there is no way the LAN can cope.

CRUCIAL TIP

It is important to remember that data is measured in megabytes (MB) and networks work in megabits (Mb). To convert you need to multiply MB by 8.

When considering placing an application on the LAN, the effects of doing so must be taken into account. If the LAN in our example was mission critical, by adding the video we would slow the information on the LAN to a trickle – which would mean the organisation would be unable to carry out its mission. This could seriously damage the organisation. For a store like Argos at Christmas, if an employee chose to watch a video over the LAN, slowing it to a trickle, it might well take 30 minutes to serve each customer! The one thing that is certain about bandwidth is that we can never have enough. An organisation's requirements will constantly grow, just as LAN capacity will grow.

CRUCIAL CONCEPT

Networks don't have unlimited capacity. When introducing applications or data to the LAN or making changes, we must ensure that the LAN can cope with the new load (see Chapter 7).

Quick test

Describe briefly what is meant by the term 'bandwidth'. Discuss why it is important to assess bandwidth and its impact when considering installing a networked application.

Section 4

Security implications

Whilst computer networks undoubtedly provide unparalleled access to information, they can also provide it to prying eyes. As soon as information is networked it is shared with people we want to share it with and those we don't want to share it with. Hence the need for security measures. (Security is given fuller treatment in Chapters 8 and 10.)

Security implications

Information security is often as paramount for commercial organisations as it is for military organisations. Companies have commercially sensitive information as well as obligations under such legislation as the Data Protection Act 1984. Before the widespread use of computers, information security was provided by rugged filing cabinets, perhaps a security guard and, usually, a personnel-screening system. The aim was simple – to limit access to sensitive information. Unauthorised access to such information could be damaging to the company. Consider a car dealership – access to customer lists would be very helpful to other dealers.

Before the widespread use of computers, it was relatively easy to spot someone stealing information – long periods spent at the photocopier and carrying large boxes of paper out of the building. The widespread use of computers makes it much easier to steal information. By using a DAT cartridge it is possible to steal 23 GB of data on a cartridge small enough to fit into a shirt pocket (to put 23GB in context – the entire *Encyclopaedia Britannica* is around 1 GB!). Essentially, anyone connected to the corporate network has access to the information held on its computers and also travelling across the network. Organisations need to take steps to protect the contents of their servers and other computers. Access to servers should be via a password only, and users should be given the minimum access rights necessary for them to carry out their work. Computers (including PCs) that are connected to a corporate network should be reviewed to ensure that only the files and directories that need to be shared are shared and that all others are protected. Again, access to shared drives should be via a password only.

CRUCIAL CONCEPT

Security should be paramount. To ignore security is to risk the organisation's entire existence – it cannot be treat piecemeal. All organisations must take a professional approach to computer security.

Quick test

Briefly discuss why security is a vitally important issue with information held on a network.

Section 5

Licensing issues

Breaking licence agreements is a civil offence, as is a breach of copyright or copying software. Software piracy is a serious issue and is reported to be costing the software industry billions of dollars each year. In 1984, the British Computer Society's Copyright Committee established the Federation Against Software Theft (or FAST). The aim of FAST is to safeguard software and, contrary to popular belief, the organisation represents both users and software producers. FAST can assist in identifying and prosecuting organisations or individuals who copy or use copied software or who breach licence agreements. Unauthorised copying of software and breaches of a software licence are serious crimes and there can be severe penalties for those caught. The network manager is often the one who is nominated to oversee an organisation's licence agreements, and such managers must understand licensing issues fully.

Licensing issues

Discussion of software licensing has necessarily been limited here. Network managers must ensure they understand their position fully and the wider issues involved. Before computer networks, licensing issues were relatively simple – a licence was bought for every machine the software was to be installed upon. If an organisation had 25 machines but only 10 were in use at any one time, it still needed 25 copies of the software or one per CPU. With the advent of computer networks, software could be held centrally and downloaded to a machine when required. Software manufacturers realised this and released appropriately designed networked versions of their software. Central to these licences is the issue of concurrency. Thus, a ten-user licence of networked software means a maximum of ten machines can be using that software at one time. When an eleventh user downloads and runs the software, this is a breach of the licence agreement. Some manufacturers include the word 'normally' in the licence agreement: 'the number of users of the software will normally not exceed x'. The intention here is that, in exceptional circumstances, they would not be averse to more users than the licence permits, although there will be restrictions. An example of this could be the student records system in your institution. Normally it may only have eight users but, during times of enrolment extra staff may be needed to cope. This term, however, does not apply to all software and its meaning should be checked with the manufacturers.

Some argue that a user logging into a network and starting a piece of networked software may be unaware that the maximum number of licences have been used and that it is the software itself that should enforce the licence agreement. The argument about the user logging in is, however, valid – an organisation should know how many people are likely to be using a piece of software at one time. For example, if a university has three classes of 25 students using Microsoft Office, it should know it needs 75 licences. Some software does, on the other hand, enforce the licensing agreement through a licence meter. This works by the software either refusing to start if the maximum number of licences has been reached or – more cruelly – logging out the user who has been connected for the longest period of time. Whilst the use of a meter sounds good in practice it can be problematic. If a machine crashes whilst using the software it may not release the licence and, when restarted, may consume another licence. Eventually, this could lead to the situation where all the licences have been consumed through faults and so no one can use the software. This would obviously lead to frustration and to increased technical support costs.

Quick test

Briefly discuss the main issues concerning software licensing.

CRUCIAL CONCEPT

An organisation must ensure it has sufficient software licences for the software in use. In the case of operating systems this will usually mean one licence per computer (as all computers need an operating system). Other software may be available in a networked version. An organisation should also ensure that the maximum number of concurrent users allowed under the licence agreement is never exceeded. Exceeding the licence agreement may result in prosecution, and the authorities take a serious view of such cases.

Section 6

End of chapter assessment

Questions

1. You have been approached by a local charity who wish to network their office. They have limited funds and have asked you to identify the minimum resources they would need to network their office. They currently run donated copies of Windows 95.

2. The charity are aiming to help the unemployed over-fifties to get to grips with computing in the hope they can find employment. Typically, they intend to train ten students at a time in the use of word processors. The charity also have a small administration team of three. Two of the team typically use Microsoft Word and Access on a daily basis, handling confidential files on the charity's students and producing references for employment. A further administrator uses Excel. The functions this team provide can be considered mission critical. As the charity do not have sufficient printing resources, they would like the administration team to be connected to the network. Outline the benefits a network would offer the charity.

3. The founder of the charity has recently acquired a 150MB AVI video which, over a period of 15 minutes, introduces the trainees to the benefits of word processing and many of the techniques they need. She feels that the class can use the video throughout the lesson rather than having formal instruction. As the charity will be networked she feels that delivery of the video over the network will be ideal and has sought your advice.

4. The charity have also asked your advice on the security implications of connecting the administrative staff to the teaching network.

5. The charity have a ten-user licence for Word which is currently used by two administrators. They wish to use the same licence for the classes they intend to teach and have asked for your advice on the licensing issues of such a move.

Answers

The questions above are all inter-related and are based upon a small case study. This is deliberate as it is likely that assessment of such topics will be in this form. Thus the answers below are likely to form subsections of your overall answer. In practice, the case study would go into far greater detail and would be tied in with capacity planning covered in Chapter 7.

1. To answer this question, you need to pick up on the key facts – the organisation is a charity and has limited funds. They are seeking your advice on the minimum resources they need to get their network operational. Obviously there are two sides to this question as it is meant to test your academic knoweldge – the assessor is not just looking for a shopping list but for a list of items the charity require together with an **explanation** of why they need it and some form of explanation of what the item actually does/a justification of why it is needed. Don't forget: for a network to be successful, you need both hardware and software and the software they have would appear to support their requirements.

2. This question is asking you to outline the benefits a computer network would bring to the charity. Although this is a case study there is considerable scope in the benefits it can provide. Again, don't forget that the assessor isn't simply looking for a list of benefits: he or she is looking to see that you understand the benefits (shown through discussion) and that the benefits you propose are realistic and achievable within the charity's limited budget.

3. This question is about managing the expectations of the end user. Networks are useful and do provide enormous benefits but they have limited bandwidth. In this example the founder of the charity has great expectations of the network which it won't be able to deliver inside of her limited budget (assuming they will install a 10 Mb coaxial ethernet network – see Chapter 5). You need to discuss the fact that networks have limited bandwidth and advise her on what is and is not realistic.

4. Although this question is simple enough the answer is more complex and, as usual in such an assessment, some of the clues are hidden elsewhere. If you review the earlier questions you will see what information is actually being held and processed on the computers connected to the network. You need to outline to the charity the security implications of what they intend to do. Again, a list isn't required – the assessor is after evidence of thought and wants to see discussion of the issues as well as guidance for the charity.

5. The answer to this question centres around software licensing issues. To answer it you need to provide a general discussion of the software licensing issues and relate this to the case of the charity. They have a networked ten-user licence for Microsoft Word but it is likely that, at peak times, they will exceed this licence. You need to inform them of the implications of this.

Section 7

Further reading and research

See the *www.PhilipIrving.com* website for up-to-date further reading and support for this chapter.

Cisco Networking Academy Program (2001) *First Year Companion Guide* (2nd edn). Cisco Press. ISBN: 1 58713 025 4. Chapters 1 and 3.

Cisco Networking Academy Program (2001) *Second Year Companion Guide* (2nd edn). Cisco Press. ISBN: 1 58713 029 7. Chapter 8.

Hodson, P. (2002) *Local Area Networks*, (4th edn). Continuum. ISBN: 0 82645 866 1. Chapters 3 and 13.

Chapter 3
Fundamentals of networks

Chapter summary

This chapter provides an introduction to computer networks and networking. When studying computer networking, it is important to understand that networking has evolved, and will continue to evolve, as the technology becomes available, and that the use to which the technology is being put and can be put will also evolve. A computer network can be categorised according to, for example, the geographical area it covers or by the access it provides to the outside world.

Learning outcomes

After studying this chapter you should aim to test your achievement of the following outcomes. You should be able to:

Outcome 1: Network basics
Understand the basics of computer networking and be familiar with some of the terms. Question 1 at the end of this chapter will test your ability to do this.

Outcome 2: Network topologies
Describe the common network topologies and be able to identify each. Question 2 at the end of this chapter will test your ability to do this.

Outcome 3: Network addressing
Understand the basics of network addressing and be able to discuss the addressing formats. Question 3 at the end of this chapter will test your ability to do this.

How will you be assessed on this?

The topics covered in this chapter form the fundamental principles of networking – how data is encoded, the different topologies and logical/physical addressing mechanisms. The most popular form of assessment for such topics is by examination or time-constrained test (TCT). The questions at the end of this chapter provide you with sample questions which may well be asked in such assessments.

Section 1

Understanding network basics

Computer networking is subject to the laws of physics, and therefore a basic understanding of the physics of networking will aid understanding. The laws of physics also govern the speed and development of networking. This section introduces some of the basic physics which impact on networking. It assumes that you understand binary – that binary is the basis of all data held and transmitted by a computer, digital signals, analogue signals and digital-to-analogue conversion. If this is not the case, it is recommended you read a book on computer architectures to pick up these basics before proceeding.

Encoding

Computer networking is about moving data (in the form of bits) along some sort of transmission media (most commonly, a piece of wire). For transmission, the data needs to be encoded into a electrical voltage which can then be carried by the wire.

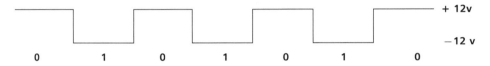

CRUCIAL TIP

Although it might seem odd, a great deal can be gleaned from comparing networking to plumbing. Here, how a wire carries data (represented by a voltage) is likened to a pipe carrying water.

Figure 3.1 shows data encoding using $+12$ v to represent a 0 and -12 v to represent a 1. It is common usage to employ two voltages to differentiate a no signal state from a signal state. Thus, if the sender is at the right and the receiver at the left, the data 0101010 is being transmitted.

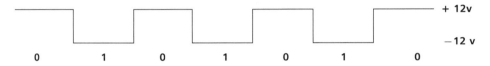

Figure 3.1   Data encoding
(diagram courtesy of Professor Peter Hodson, University of Glamorgan)

Any good computer architecture book will detail how alphanumeric characters are encoded using an encoding mechanism such as the American Std Code for Info Interchange (ASCII)

Circuits

To carry data a circuit is required. In most cases a circuit comprises two wires. Consider Figure 3.2, which is a simple torch circuit. Here, when the switch is closed, the electrons move, providing electricity to the bulb which lights up. Opening the switch stops the flow of electrons and the light goes out. This circuit could be used to represent basic binary digits (either 1 (on) or 0 (off)).

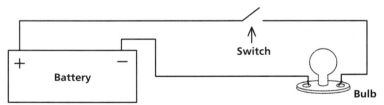

Figure 3.2   Simple torch circuit

Networking also needs complete circuits – we call the cables the 'signal' and the signal 'ground'. As can be seen from Figure 3.1, determining the height of the signal (the voltage) accurately is of crucial importance. The signal wire carries the signal whilst the signal ground completes the circuit and allows the height of the signal to be determined. In practice, networks often use multiple voltage levels to represent many bit patterns. For example, by using four voltages we can encode two bits to each voltage:

Voltage 1   00
Voltage 2   01
Voltage 3   10
Voltage 4   11

Three types of circuits are commonly used in networking:

- **Simplex** – can carry signals in one direction only (e.g. a one-way street).
- **Half duplex** – can carry signals in both ways but only one way at a time (e.g. a narrow bridge where traffic from only one direction can cross at a time – under traffic light control).
- **Full duplex** – carries signals in both directions simultaneously (e.g. dual carriage-way).

CRUCIAL TIP

You must understand these three types of circuits, as they are often referred to in a range of networking situations.

Signal problems

Electrical signals are susceptible to a wide range of interference. For example, as the signal travels along the wire it loses some of its strength and arrives at the destination weaker (a lower voltage), which makes it more difficult to determine how it was originally encoded – hence the big difference in the voltage levels used to represent a 0 and a 1. This loss of strength is known as **attenuation** and limits the distance a signal can travel without being amplified or regenerated. Attenuation can be addressed in analogue networks by amplifying the signal or, in digital networks, by repeating or regenerating the signal. Repeating is preferable as the signal generated by repeating is a perfect signal like the original, whereas amplifying also amplifies noise.

CRUCIAL TIP

Assessors quite like the topic of sources of error as an examination question.

The following is a summary of the common sources of error:

- **Attenuation**   As the signal travels along the cable it becomes weaker. On long-distance runs, unless it is aided, the signal received can be too weak to use. On 100BaseT ethernet, it is recommended that the cable lengths be no more than 100 m.
- **Impulse noise**   Sometimes known as electromagnetic interference (EMI), electrical signals given off by some electrical devices (e.g. fluorescent lights and electrical motors) can cause severe degradation to the signal or even destroy it. Lightning is also a cause of impulse noise. Care should be taken when routing the network cable to avoid close contact with such devices.
- **Thermal noise**   Thermal noise is the interference that comes from the cable itself – the distortion caused by moving the electrons. Very little can be done to address this.
- **Crosstalk**   Crosstalk is when two or more pairs of cables lying near each other interfere with the signals on the other cable. This used to be common on older telephone networks where you could hear someone else's conversation if you were quiet. Crosstalk can be largely eliminated by twisting the two wires in the circuit together.
- **Intermodulation noise**   Similar to crosstalk except that, here, the signals which interfere are being transmitted on the same cable (see Broadband/baseband below). A good example of this in the UK is Channel 5 TV which is transmitted on a frequency used by most video recorders – if the video and Channel 5 are on together they often interfere with each other. This problem can be addressed by altering the frequencies used for transmission.
- **Radiation**   Just as atmospheric conditions interfere with TV signals, they can also interfere with computer networks and telephone networks. Thankfully, such interference is rare and can be addressed by using shielded cabling.

- **Radio frequency interference** (RFI)   RFI is interference caused by devices emitting radio signals in the proximity of the network cable. Again, electric motors and flourescent lights can be a source of this. Other sources include mobile phones and other devices which transmit radio signals. Reduction of such interference is identical to impulse noise.
- **Signal reflection**   If a network cable is not terminated correctly, the transmitted signal is reflected back from the open end of the cable and interferes with the remainder of the signal and others that follow. This was a particular problem with 10Base2 and 10Base5 networks.

Electrostatic discharge (ESD)

Often referred to simply as 'static' or 'static electricity', ESD is caused by the electrons becoming loosened and staying in one place, where they look for an opportunity to 'jump' to a conductor. ESD is the shock we feel when we have built up a charge from, for example, dragging our feet on a nylon carpet and then touching something – perhaps a metal stair banister. Other than a shock, it is usually harmless to human beings but, to sensitive electronic components such as those found inside a computer or networking devices, it can be fatal. ESD can be as high as 40 000 volts which can wreak havoc on a 5-volt computer circuit.

Broadband/baseband

A TV aerial cable carries many channels (for example, BBC1 and ITV). Although there is only one piece of cable the companies are able to transmit the channels using discrete frequencies – a different frequency for each channel. Technically, this is known as **broadband signalling**.

Computer networks can operate in a similar fashion – the available frequency range of the cable can be divided up and used to transmit different signals. Broadband services from telecommunications companies use this concept – one channel for Internet access and other, separate channels for telephones and (sometimes) fax. Thus a device needs to be employed at the socket to divide the signals.

Alternatively, a signal can occupy the entire frequency range, which is known as **baseband signalling**. This allows the signal to use all the frequency range available on the cable and, hence, it has a higher throughput (more bandwidth). Ethernet uses this principle.

Packets

Data to be transmitted across the network is broken down into chunks known as **packets**. There are two main reasons for breaking the data down into chunks. To

- reduce the amount of data lost to noise; and
- ensure fair access to the medium.

───────── CRUCIAL TIP ─────────

Remember, data is measured in megabytes (MB) and data on a network is measured in megabits (Mb).

Let's imagine we need to transmit 2 Mb of data – 2 × 8 gives us 16 Mb. Let us assume that, on average, the network can transmit only 2 Mb before an error occurs. Thus we could never transmit the data as a 16 Mb entity successfully – each transmission will be corrupted by an error and require retransmission. If we break the data into packets of, say, .5 Mb each, on average we will successfully transmit three packets before an error occurs, requiring only .5 Mb to be retransmitted. By reducing the size of the packet we can prevent even more data loss. However, as each packet needs to contain the sender and receiver addresses and some mechanism for detecting errors, if we reduce the packet size too much these overheads will also reduce performance. For this and other reasons, packet size is fixed by network technology designers and cannot be altered by the user.

Breaking data into packets also provides a fairer way of sharing the medium – users each send a packet at a time rather than 'hogging' the medium until their transmission is over.

Error detection/correction

We cannot prevent errors from occurring in data transmission and it is imperative we detect all errors, since data with an error must not be used. Consider a spreadsheet with financial information – if an error has occurred we don't know that the amounts are correct and so it is unsafe to use the data. You will most likely have studied parity as an error detection method in the past. Parity is one method of error detection but it is not accurate enough for today's networks because it does not detect all errors. Instead, we use Cyclic Redundancy Checks (CRCs) based on 32 bit polynomials to detect errors. All that needs to be known is that they detect 99.997% of all errors and that correction requires the data to be retransmitted.

Quick test

1. Briefly describe how data can be sent over a computer network. Your answer should include encoding.

2. Describe the differences between full duplex, half duplex and simplex circuits.

3. Briefly describe the kinds of interference that can occur in computer networks and how these can be addressed.

Section 2

Network topologies

The words 'technology' and 'topology' are often used when discussing networks, and it is important to clarify these terms. Technologies are the hardware devices and their operation, whereas topology is the physical shape of the network. Different technologies require different topologies. In this section, the differing topologies available for computer networks are discussed, and the differences between logical and physical topology are distinguished.

CRUCIAL TIP

Naming and drawing diagrams of various networking topologies is a popular type of examination question. Examiners may also ask you to discuss which topologies support a networking technology (see Chapter 5).

Early star networks

In Chapter 1, we discussed the ways that local interactive terminals were connected to the mainframe computer – each had its own cable running back to the central computer forming a star pattern (the star network – see Figure 3.3).

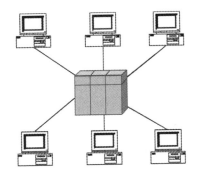

Figure 3.3   An early star network

Such cabling resulted in hundreds of cables descending upon the main computer and was costly in terms of cable and labour. Organisations often encountered problems in handling the sheer volume of cables, and relocating the central computer was a major issue.

The advantages of this type of topology, on the other hand, are:

- **robustness** – a cable break will only affect one machine;
- **performance** – each terminal has a dedicated cable.

RS232-C connectors (Figure 3.4) are the standard connectors used here (known as D.25). The cable used is twisted pair (see Figure 3.19).

Figure 3.4   D.25 serial connector

Point-to-point network

The point-to-point network is the simplest of all topologies. In the point-to-point topology (Figure 3.5), two computers are connected together via a physical wire. It is a network because it has networking hardware and software to facilitate the exchange of information. However, normally the overheads of a two-station network are greater than the benefits. Costing less than £30 at early 2003 prices (when based on ethernet technology – see Chapter 5), this topology is useful in small organisations or the home where two computers perhaps share costly resources, such as a colour laser printer, or to facilitate file transfer.

Figure 3.5   Point-to-point network

Bus network

The bus network (Figure 3.6) used to be very common and was used by a number of technologies – most notably, ethernet. In this topology a central 'backbone' cable spans the area and computers 'tap' into this backbone for their connection. In a bus network, the communications medium is shared between the computers attached to it.

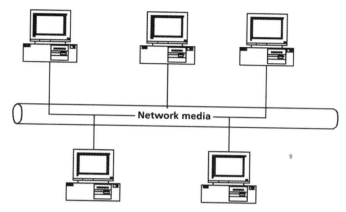

Figure 3.6   Bus network

The advantages of a bus network include the following:

- They are easy and inexpensive to install.
- It is easy to add further devices by tapping into the wire (avoiding the costs of expensive recabling).
- Bandwidth was higher than early star networks.
- Facilitates communication with the interconnected device without going through the central computer.

The disadvantages included the following:

- The media was shared – therefore there was contention for access which required an algorithm to ensure fairness.
- Data was sent in a broadcast fashion, meaning that all computers could 'see' the information.
- A cable break on the main bus cable took down the entire network.
- Although the cable was higher capacity, it was shared amongst many more users. As network traffic increased, capacity became an issue.

This kind of toplogy was popular (along with ring and tree networks) from the mid-1980s until around 1992, when the volume of network traffic started to increase dramatically and performance became an issue.

For cabling and connectors, see tree networks.

Tree network

It is possible to connect bus networks together to form a bus network that has branches with other bus networks. Such a topology is known as a tree network (Figure 3.7). As it is essentially a bus network, a tree network has the same advantages and disadvantages as a standard bus network. The devices used at the joints are known as **hubs** and are a specialist piece of hardware. The standard connector used in this type of network was the British Naval Connector (BNC) (Figure 3.8). The cable used was co-axial cable (similar to that used by TV aerials and cable TV) (Figure 3.9).

Figure 3.7   Tree network

Figure 3.8   British naval connector (BNC)

Figure 3.9   Coaxial cable
(diagram courtesy of Professor Peter Hodson, University of Glamorgan)

Ring network

In the ring topology (Figure 3.10), computers are connected to one another in a circular fashion and therefore form a ring. Although several companies and several implementations were involved, the two most notable were the Cambridge ring (developed in Cambridge University and used extensively by Acorn in the BBC microcomputer series) and the Token Ring (developed and used extensively by IBM). The dominant network in this topology was IBM's Token Ring network.

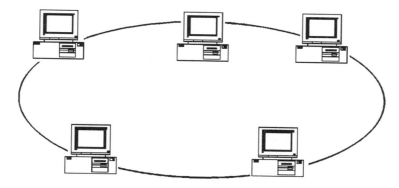

Figure 3.10   Ring network

The advantages of the ring topology are as follows:

- Robustness – there are two links to each PC.
- In the case of the Token Ring, higher capacity than standard ethernet.
- A fairer method of access than standard ethernet (see Chapter 5).

The major disadvantage was cost. As the equipment used in the topology was IBM propriety technology (which had a royalty fee attached to it), it was substantially more expensive than bus networks. Eventually, the ethernet gained the lion's share of the market (due to costs) and later versions of the ethernet outstripped the ring network's capacity.

Star with logical ring

Occasionally, ring networks (especially IBM's Token Ring) appear to be a star network (Figure 3.11) as they run to a piece of hardware called a multistation access unit (MAU). This essentially connects all the computers together and gives the network a star appearance. However, the network is still very much a ring and operates as such.

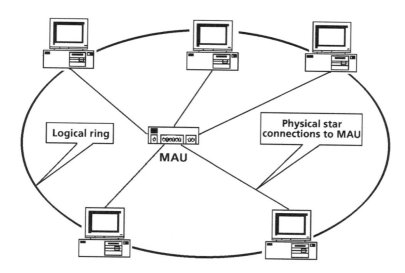

Figure 3.11   Logical ring

Connectors used in the IBM Token Ring are a proprietary technology (Figure 3.12), although most are now RJ-45. The cable used was shielded twisted pair (Figure 3.13). Shielded RJ-45 connectors are also commonly used with this technology (Figure 3.14).

Figure 3.12   Typical Token Ring connectors

Figure 3.13   STP cabling (diagram courtesy of Peter Hodson, University of Glamorgan)

Figure 3.14   STP RJ-45 connector (note the metal grounding)

Mesh network

The final topology is the mesh network (Figure 3.15). With a mesh network, a number of connections exist between machines and, in order to get from one machine to another, a route must be established. Mesh networks are complex and are designed to provide resilience in the event of a cable break. A mesh network can be either full or partial. In the case of a full mesh network, every node is directly connected to every other node – there is more than one route to every PC or network in the mesh. As its name suggests, a partial mesh network is not complete (Figure 3.15 shows a full mesh network). The Internet itself is a mesh network, as part of its original design specification was resilience. The major advantage of mesh networks is resilience, and the major disadvantages are cost and complexity. Mesh networks are almost always WAN links and, therefore, the cabling is by the service provider. A typical connector (V.35) is shown in Fig 3.16.

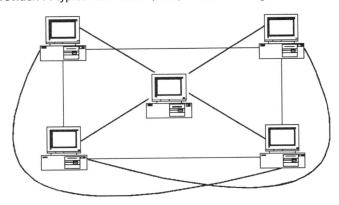

Figure 3.15   Full mesh network

Figure 3.16   Typical WAN serial connector (V.35)

Structured cabling solutions/modern star

Modern organisations experience a great deal of change during their lifetimes and have high demands for networks in terms of capacity and reliability. The original star network offered capacity that was dedicated to a terminal and that was extremely robust. Because of these advantages, the star network has been developed further and remains the preferred solution for modern cabling. A modern star network (see Figure 3.17) has, at its centre, a wiring closet to which all communications points (telephone sockets, computer sockets, etc.) on that floor are connected. Inside the wiring closet, each connection terminates in a patch panel which can then be connected to a service using a patch lead. Services would typically include different computer networks, telephone services and perhaps ISDN lines.

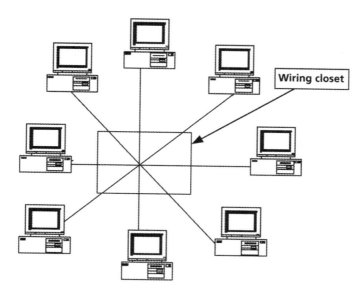

Figure 3.17   Modern star network

Known as a structured cabling solution, this is the recommended wiring structure for new installations, each installation requiring one wiring closet per 1000 m² floor interconnected by cable (usually fibre), known as backbone cabling. Structured cabling specifications require a minimum of two connection points to be installed per user and provide a very flexible communications solution. Figure 3.18 shows a typical structured cabling solution. The PC is connected through an interface card (see Chapter 5) via a 'drop cable' to the floor socket. This is connected directly to the patch panel in the wiring closet. A patch lead then 'patches' the required service from the service point to the patch panel. In this case, the service is an ethernet network. The standards for structured cabling recommend that Category 5 unshielded twisted pair (UTP) cabling (Figure 3.19) is used throughout the installation, terminated by RJ-45 plugs (Figure 3.20) and sockets.

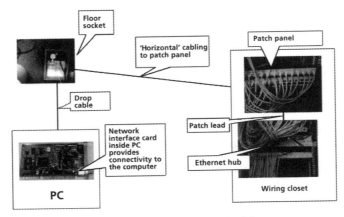

Figure 3.18   Typical structured cabling

Figure 3.19   UTP cabling (diagram courtesy of CISCO Systems Inc.)

Figure 3.20   RJ-45 connector

──────────── CRUCIAL TIP ────────────

Structured cabling is now the standard in almost all new installations.

──────────── CRUCIAL CONCEPT ────────────

It is important to be able to remember the various topologies and to be able to draw these topologies.

Technologies

As well as having a physical shape, networks also need equipment in order for them to operate – for example, a network interface card (NIC), hub, etc. The equipment to support a network is known collectively as the technology (examples being the ethernet and token ring). The most popular technologies are discussed in detail in Chapter 5.

Quick test

1. Name the most common network topologies and discuss the differences between them.

2. For each of the topologies given, list any advantages/disadvantages.

Section 3

Network addressing and protocols

Computer networking is a complex business and requires rules to govern the communication. Such rules are known as protocols and are critical to computer networking. Most crucial of all is the open systems interconnection (OSI) seven-layer model for computer communication, which defines standards and protocols that are used extensively in the networking industry today.

Protocols

Computer communications are extremely complex, and there are many parameters that must be agreed before communication can take place. What was needed, therefore, was a standard (or protocol) for communication between computers. In other areas, this problem has been resolved by breaking down one large, complex problem into several smaller ones – for instance, with personal CD players the headphone jack is 3.5 mm, therefore, any headphones can be used; any audio-compatible CD played on a personal CD machine; any make of batteries can be used; and, if the player has a mains adaptor, it can be plugged into any mains outlet. This is because tight standards have been set that govern the production of all the pieces of equipment.

The same is true with networking: standards for networks were established and a model devised. This model, known as the open systems interconnection (OSI) seven-layer model, was devised by members of ISO (the International Standards Organisation). The layers of the OSI seven-layer model are shown in Figure 3.21, and the model is discussed in detail in Chapter 4. Prior to the model (which was devised in the early 1980s), vendors tended to produce proprietary network solutions, which reduced the end user's choice and limited the connectivity of the machine.

| Application |
| Presentation |
| Session |
| Transport |
| Network |
| Data link |
| Physical |

Figure 3.21   The ISO seven-layer model

The benefits the layered model brings are as follows:

- It breaks network communication down into smaller simpler parts that are easier to develop.
- It facilitates the standardisation of network components to allow multi-vendor development and support.
- It allows different types of hardware and software to communicate with each other.
- It prevents changes in one layer from affecting the other layers so that they can be developed more quickly.
- It makes networks easier to learn.

Whilst the seven-layer model brings many benefits, it has several disadvantages:

- Redundant functions and facilities are retained.
- Simple communication is made over-complicated because of structure overheads.
- The structure overheads reduce the overall performance.

CRUCIAL TIP

Apart from their importance in the real world of networking, the benefits and disadvantages of layered approaches to networking is a very common question in TCTs.

Logical and physical addressing

Devices on a network must be able to communicate directly with one another and must be uniquely identified. Communication can then take place in a way similar to the postal system: the sender addresses an envelope or package to a recipient (including a return address). The postal system examines the recipient's address and forwards the package as appropriate. This may involve the package being forwarded to another postal network or sorting office before being delivered to the recipient.

Computer networks operate on an almost identical principle. Each machine on the network has an address to which data can be forwarded. In order to reach its recipient, the package may have to cross multiple networks before it is delivered. On a computer, there are two possible addressing mechanisms:

- physical
- logical.

Physical addressing (also known as layer two addressing as it occurs in layer two of the model) mechanisms are used internally within an organisation. They use an address that is hardcoded on to the Media Access Control unit (MAC) – usually part of the networking card (i.e. the NIC). With ethernet networks, this is either a 16 or 48 bit field (usually the latter) that is unique across the world. Burnt into ROM and unable to be changed, the first half of the address identifies the manufacturer; the second half is the serial number within the manufacturer's ID. Thus replacing a card will change the MAC address. Whilst this is acceptable for local area networks where the address is circulated as the machine interacts, it would clearly be impossible to know the physical address of every machine in the world (and to keep that list up to date!). Thus another mechanism for addressing machines globally is needed – logical.

Logical addressing is used for three main reasons. To:

1. overcome the problem of a card change;
2. allow the demarcation of networks;
3. provide a structure to the addressing scheme.

The best analogy that can be drawn to logical addressing is the telephone network. If you purchased a phone and the serial number of that phone was your phone number, each time you changed the phone you would need to notify all your friends of your new number – something that is clearly undesirable. Also, as phones could be located anywhere in the world, when friends call the network would have to try every phone in the world to find out if it was yours – a huge waste of resources. Instead, the telephone network is structured. For example if you were to ring the University of Sunderland from outside the UK you would dial the following number:

00 44 191 5153000

The 00 routes the call from the local telephone exchange to an international one; the 44 routes the call to the UK; the 191 to the north east of England; the 515 to the University of Sunderland; and the 3000 is the number of the student helpline. This structure allows the telephone network to make much better use of its resources, and it allows demarcation of telephone networks – once the call has left one country/service provider it is the responsibility of another. Also, you can change your phone at will without having to notify your friends.

Logical addressing for networks is very similar. The most popular logical addressing mechanism is that used on the Internet – Internet Protocol (IP) addressing. With IP addressing, an organisation is issued a block of IP addresses from its Internet Service Provider (ISP), who is issued these by the Network Information Center in the USA (early in Internet development, the Network Info. Center would issue blocks of numbers, known as licences, directly to large organisations – see below). These numbers are 4 byte dotted decimal. For example:

157.228.102.1

CRUCIAL CONCEPT

We need to use logical addressing to provide a means by which we can structure traffic on the Internet and maintain independence from the MAC address.

Computers are thus grouped under the organisation's or ISP's network address, which are issued in licenses. Although these numbers are dotted decimal, they are actually a decimal representation of eight binary digits (a byte). The largest number that can be represented by a byte is 255 (all 0s are reserved for the network address and all 1s are reserved for the broadcast address; therefore the maximum available is 254). There are three possible types of licence:

- **Class A licences**   These were intended for very large organisations and were mainly issued to universities in the US. In a class A licence, the first byte is fixed but the organisation is free to allocate addresses in the other bytes, giving it a maximum of $254 \times 254 \times 254 = 16.3$ million possible addresses on its network. Class A licences are no longer issued. In a class A licence, the leftmost bit is always zero. The largest number that can be represented is therefore 127 and thus the range is: 1–126. $X. X. X$ (127 is reserved for the loopback address – a means of testing the network hardware and software on a computer).
- **Class B licences**   These were also issued to large organisations – many universities in the UK hold a class B licence. With a class B licence, the first two bytes are fixed, giving the organisation a maximum of $254 \times 254 = 64\,516$ possible addresses on its network. Thus 157.228 uniquely identifies the University of Sunderland; the remaining parts of the address identify specific machines. Class B licences are very rarely issued now. The first two bits of a class B licence are always 10. Therefore the effective range is 128–191. $X. X. X.$

- **Class C licences** These are the most common and are still issued. In a class C licence, the first three bytes are fixed, giving the organisation 254 possible addresses on its network. The first three bits if a class C licence are always 110 therefore the effective range is 192–223. *X. X. X.*

Internet service providers (ISPs) either allocate IP addresses statically – that is to say, a machine always has the same IP address (a necessity for a web server), or dynamically – leased for a period (usually 24 hours), after which it needs to be reviewed. Logical addressing is also known as layer-three addressing because it occurs at layer-three of the OSI seven-layer model.

Subnetworks (subnets)

As can be seen from the above, with class A and B licences there would be a huge number of hosts on a network. If we take class A as an example, it is possible there could be 16.3 million computers on a single network. This is akin to having all the cars in the country on one road at the same time – there would be too much traffic and everything would grind to a halt. Just as the road network comprises many roads, the computer network can also be divided into smaller networks or subnetworks (often referred to as subnets). And just as with road networks, such a division reduces the load in each subnetwork enabling traffic to flow more freely. The key to good network design is traffic management (see Chapter 7).

The network is therefore divided using a subnetwork (or subnet) mask. As its name suggests, this is a mask (in the form of 4 bytes) that is applied to the IP number to determine the correct network for the traffic. The subnet mask is local to the organisation only (i.e. it is not transmitted outside the organisation) and is found in a computer's settings. In Windows this can be found in the Network Connections box or by running ipconfig (Windows XP and 2000) or winipcfg (in Windows 98) (Figure 3.22).

Figure 3.22   Ethernet settings (winipcfg in Windows 98)

In this example, we can see that the IP address is class B (157 is in the class B range). Where there is a value other than zero in the subnet mask, the corresponding part of the IP address is treated as part of the network. Each part of the IP address is a byte (with a maximum value of 255) – thus in the figure the subnet mask identifies that all the first, second and third bytes of the IP address relate to the network. Thus, host 121 is to be found on subnetwork 102 of major network 157.228 (see Chapter 11 for an example).

Section 4

End of chapter assessment

Questions

1. Discuss how data is encoded on to a medium and why a packet structure is used. You should use any necessary diagrams to illustrate your answer.
2. For each popular networking topology, draw a diagram illustrating the topology and highlight any advantages/disadvantages of the topology.
3. Discuss the terms 'logical' and 'physical' addressing. Highlight any differences and give an example of the use of each.

Answers

1. This question tests your knowledge of network basics. The assessor is trying to find out if you understand the fundamentals of computer communications – that we need to encode data as a voltage for transmission, that we use at least two voltages (and why); and that a packet structure is necessary. To answer it, you need to discuss how data is encoded on to the medium and why a packet structure is used. Wherever possible, you should illustrate your answer with diagrams.
2. Topologies are a common question and come in a variety of guises. Once you have learnt the topologies, tackling such a question is fairly easy – all you need to do is to draw a diagram of each of the topologies and to list their advantages and disadvantages. Drawing the diagrams is an essential part of the answer.
3. This particular question is trying to establish whether you know about the addressing mechanisms used in computer networking. The ideal answer to this question would discuss both terms separately, highlight any differences between them and discuss why these differences are necessary. You should illustrate your answer with examples of both addressing mechanisms and, for extra marks, highlight why the Internet could not run with physical addressing mechanisms. Comparing addressing schemes to either the postal service or the telephone network will impress the assessor and will earn you extra marks.

Section 5

Further reading and research

See the *www.PhilipIrving.com* website for up-to-date further reading and support for this chapter.

Cisco Networking Academy Program (2001) *First Year Companion Guide* (2nd edn) Cisco Press. ISBN: 1 58713 025 4. Chapters 1, 3 and 10.

Hodson, P. (2002) *Local Area Networks* (4th edn) Continuum. ISBN: 0 82645 866 1. Chapters 6 and 7.

Chapter 4
Standards

Chapter summary

One of the most important things to understand when studying networking are the standards involved. The main set of standards that has helped networks evolve so quickly is the Open Systems Integration (OSI) seven-layer model. This provides a model for the development of computer communication and is fundamental to the study of networking. Other models exist, however, the two most important being the transmission control protocol/Internet protocol model and the Novell netware model. TCP/IP is of great importance as the Internet is built around this model; the netware model, however, is seen as less important in the networking industry today. This chapter concentrates on the OSI and TCP/IP models. (The benefits of the seven-layer model were discussed in Chapter 3.)

Learning outcomes

After studying this chapter you should aim to test your achievement of the following outcomes. You should be able to:

Outcome 1: OSI seven-layer model
Understand the concept of, and each layer of, the OSI seven-layer model. Question 1 at the end of this chapter will test your ability to do this.

Outcome 2: TCP/IP model
Understand the TCP/IP model and each of its layers. Question 2 at the end of this chapter will test your ability to do this.

Outcome 3: Comparison of the models
Understand the differences and similarities between the OSI seven-layer model and the TCP/IP model. Question 3 at the end of this chapter will test your ability to do this.

How will you be assessed on this?

Of all the topics in networking, assessors feel obliged to assess your knowledge of this subject – the study of these models is like the study of the human body to medicine! Assessment usually takes place in an exam or TCT – the subject lends itself well to this. I have written over 30 papers in the last eight years and all have had at least one question on these models!

CRUCIAL TIP

This chapter is probably the most important in this book, and understanding it is key to the study of networking. *You should study this chapter repeatedly until you understand it.* This study shouldn't be in vain – you are almost guaranteed to be assessed on it. This is even more true of MCSE or CCNA professional qualifications.

Section 1

The OSI seven-layer model

Early computer networking evolved slowly and in a proprietary fashion until those bodies involved in networking came together under the umbrella of the International Standards Organisation (ISO) and developed the open systems interconnection (OSI) model. This model has been responsible for the rapid development of computer networking that has taken place and which continues to take place. Understanding the seven-layer model is an absolute necessity for the continued study of networking and for most professional qualifications.

The OSI seven-layer model

The OSI seven-layer model (sometimes referred to as the ISO seven-layer model) basically divides the complex process of computer communication into smaller, tightly defined parts that aid understanding and network development (the benefits of a layered approach are discussed in Chapter 3). Because the process is broken into parts, it provides opportunities for vendors to specialise in particular areas of networking rather than offering a complete service. This is common practice in other areas (for example, as we saw in Chapter 3, with portable CD players). The layers of the OSI seven-layer model were given in Figure 3.21 in the last chapter but are shown here again for convenience in Figure 4.1.

Application
Presentation
Session
Transport
Network
Data link
Physical

Figure 4.1   The OSI seven-layer model

CRUCIAL TIP

A phrase might help you remember the order of the layers in the model. My personal favourite (which works from the bottom up) is:

Please
Do
Not
Throw
Sausage
Pizza
Away

There is another – '**A P**owered-down **S**ystem **T**ransmits **N**o **D**ata **P**ackets' – which works top down.

The seven-layer model facilitates communication between any two computer systems that support the model even though their underlying architecture, encoding mechanisms (e.g. ASCII, EBCDIC) and method of storage are totally incompatible. The model therefore allows totally incompatible machines (such as Apple MACs and PCs) to share data, to send email and to browse the web. The model achieves this by converting the data into an abstract data type that can be understood by both machine types and through handling all aspects of communication between the machines.

To take an abstract example. A French businessman wishes to speak to a Greek businesswoman over the phone. Neither can speak the language of the other and so they decide to use interpreters. Unfortunately, they cannot find a French-to-Greek interpreter in either country but can find a French-to-English in France and a Greek-to-English in Greece. By using the abstract language of English they have a basis for communication. They also need to establish the call (through the company telephone operator), to have mechanisms in place to redial should the connection break, to speak courteously, etc. They may also need to handle delays in the telephone network. Figure 4.2 shows how such a communication structure might look.

Figure 4.2 Communicating using telephones

As can be appreciated, this process is quite complex: the business people don't need to know how the telephone networks operate or how the telephone operates, the language of the other person or even the number to dial. They simply rely on services provided by the others but the services must meet standards. The seven-layer model uses the same concept for computer communication, although the functions of each layer are clearly different.

The upper layers

The top three layers of the model are application orientated – that is, they are machine and operating-system specific, converting the data received from the network into a usable form and vice versa.

Layer 7: the application layer
The application layer is the network layer that is closest to the user. It differs from the other layers in that it doesn't provide services to any other OSI layer. It provides the user's application (for example, browsers, telnet, word processors, spreadsheets) with network services, such as file access, Internet access and shared printing. One of the best ways of

remembering the application layer and its function is to think of it as the interface for browsers.

Layer 6: the presentation layer

The presentation layer is responsible for converting between data formats – putting the data to be sent into an abstract form and converting data received into a format suitable for the machine. The presentation layer is also responsible for data compression and is associated with such formats as JPEG, GIF and applications such as Quicktime. The easiest way to remember it is to think of it as the English-to-French translator.

Layer 5: the session layer

The session layer is responsible for establishing, managing and terminating sessions between two communicating hosts. It also provides for the synchronisation of dialogue between the hosts, for session regulation, efficient data transfer, class of service and exception reporting. Effectively the session layer controls the dial-up box which springs up when we attempt to use the Internet without having a connection. It also controls dialogues and conversations.

The lower layers

So far we have been discussing information to be sent as data. As discussed in Chapter 3, the data, however, must be broken down into packets to be transmitted effectively across the network. It is in the lower layers that the data enters the process of being broken down. Hence, the lower layers of the model are concerned with data transport, whereas the upper three layers are concerned with application issues. This boundary can be thought of as that between application protocols and data-flow protocols.

Layer 4: the transport layer

The transport layer breaks the data from the sending host down into units called **segments** and reassembles the segments received into data. This layer also provides the session layer with a transport service and shields it from details such as reliability and flow control. To provide a reliable service, transport error detection, error recovery and information flow control are used (think of flow control and reliability for ease of memory).

Layer 3: the network layer

The network layer is a complex layer where logical addressing resides. It is the layer that provides connectivity and path selection between the host systems. The Internet operates at this layer. The devices in it (often represented by the 'cloud' in diagrams) switch the data packets to the appropriate path using the logical address (that is known as routing – see Chapters 6 and 11). These hosts can be on geographically separate networks.

The data continues to be broken up. In this layer, the segments are broken into packets suitable for transmission across the Internet. Headers and tailers are added to the packets to make them suitable for transmission. The most important elements in the header are the destination address (the network address of the destination machine) and the source address (the network address of the sending machine). Nowadays these addresses are almost always IP addresses – and we can think of them as such (see Chapter 3 for more information on IP addresses). The most important element in the tailer is the CRC (see Chapter 3). Note that the size of the data is increasing as we add the headers and footers. (To remember this layer, think of path selection, routing and logical addressing.)

Layer 2: the data link layer

The data link layer provides for the transit of data across a physical link. As it is the physical link it uses physical addresses. These addresses are particular to the networking technology in use – i.e. we are now becoming network dependent. Whilst the technology itself embraces this layer, it and also covers access to the communications medium (see Chapter 5).

The data continues to be broken up. The packets are taken from the network layer and are broken into frames suitable for transmission over the implemented network technology. Different network technologies – for example, ethernet and token ring (see Chapter 5) – have different frame sizes and composition – just as the envelopes used for letters differ in size between the USA and the UK. Again, headers and footers are added to the data. The headers contain the physical addresses of the source and destination machines, and the tailer contains another CRC for the frame. (To remember this layer, think of frames and access control.)

Layer 1: the physical layer

The physical layer is the very bottom of the model and is concerned with the electrical, mechanical, procedural and functional specifications for activating, maintaining and deactivating the physical link between end systems. The data is sent from this layer one bit at a time, perhaps as voltages on a wire. Thus the data needs to be broken up into further bits at this layer of the model. The properties that allow the data to be sent and received accurately (such as voltage levels, timing of voltage changes, physical data rates, etc.) need to be defined here. Maximum transmission distances, physical connectors and other similar attributes are defined in this layer's specification. (The best way to remember this layer is to think of physical properties and bits.)

CRUCIAL TIP

In this discussion of the seven-layer model we have looked at five distinct formats in which the data is converted or encapsulated. From the bottom up these are:

• bits
• frames
• packets
• segments
• data stream.

Again, a phrase might help you to remember this. My favourite is:

British
Forces
Postal
Service

The data simply comes at the end!

Quick test

List the seven layers of the OSI seven-layer model and briefly describe each. Now adjust your answer to show how the data is encapsulated at each later.

CRUCIAL TIP

The seven-layer model will almost certainly crop up as an examination question at some point. The model is so fundamental to networking that an examiner is almost duty bound to ask it! You may as well, therefore, make life simple and learn it thoroughly now.

Section 2

The TCP/IP model

Although the OSI model is recognised and used universally, the open standard for the Internet is transmission control protocol/Internet protocol. TCP/IP makes data communication possible between two computers (running appropriate software) anywhere in the world at almost the speed of electricity (consider emails). The US Department of Defense (DoD) design specification for the Internet was for a computer network that allowed military bases to communicate across the world and which was also capable of surviving a war (including a nuclear war). Thus the Internet is a mesh network (see Chapter 3) with multiple paths to each location to allow the data packets to get through every time under any conditions. This presented challenges for the designers (remember the Internet was developed in the late 1960s) who went on to develop a four-layer model (see Figure 4.3). It is important to bear the original intention of the Internet in mind as we examine this model.

Figure 4.3   The TCP/IP model

CRUCIAL TIP

Just as it is useful to have a mnemnoic to help remember the order of the layers of the seven-layer model, so it is useful to have one for the TCP/IP model. I remember the UNIX model as simply:

A TIN

Application layer

The designers of the Internet opted to create a layer that could handle all the higher or application-orientated protocols. Thus the application layer (sometimes referred to as the process layer) handles high-level data protocols, issues of representation, encoding and dialogue control. Just like the seven-layer model, this layer ensures the data is properly packaged for the next layer.

Transport layer

Also known as the host-to-host layer, the transport layer is in the same place in this model as it is in the seven-layer model. As with the seven-layer model, data is segmented within this layer ready for the next layer. The transport layer provides some of the protocols that are used to send data across the Internet. Specifically, it provides the Transmission Control Protocol (TCP) which supports connection-orientated services such as File Transfer Protocol (FTP), Hypertext Transfer Protocol (HTTP), Simple Mail Transfer Protocol (SMTP) and Domain Name Services (DNS) (for domain name lookups). It also provides a connectionless service known as UDP (User Datagram Protocol) which provides a faster but unreliable service. Generally UDP is used for trivial FTP (TFTP) and sometimes DNS.

Internet layer

This is best thought of as the postal service that delivers the letters (or, in this case, packets) you send. Segments are accepted from the transport layer and converted into packets. It allows these packets to be transmitted from any network on the Internet so they arrive at their destination independent of the path and networks it took to get there. The best route must be selected at this layer (e.g. it mustn't select a link which is down), which is known as **path determination**. The placing of the data on to the link is known as **switching**. **Routers** (see Chapter 6) handle these tasks. The Internet Layer is roughly equivalent to the network layer of the seven-layer model.

Network access layer

This layer is essentially a combination of the seven-layer model's physical and data link layers. As such it is concerned with all the issues an IP packet requires to cross a physical link from one device to another, directly connected device. This is sometimes called the host-to-network layer. Data encapsulation into frames and bits is also handled by this layer.

CRUCIAL CONCEPT

Learn the TCP/IP model thoroughly as it is also fundamental to networking and crucial for further studies, such as Cisco or Microsoft professional.

Quick test

List the four layers of the TCP/IP model and briefly describe each one.

Section 3

Comparison of the models

The OSI seven-layer model and the TCP/IP model perform a similar function in that they allow any connected computers to communicate. Figure 4.4 compares the seven-layer model and the TCP/IP model.

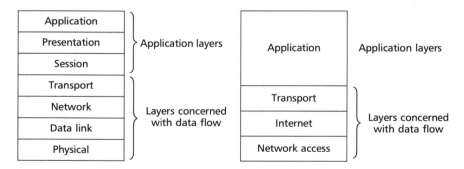

Figure 4.4   Comparison of the OSI seven-layer model and the TCP/IP model

The similarities between the two models can be summarised as follows:

- Both are layered models and, as such, have the benefits of layering (see Chapter 3).
- Both have application layers, although the TCP/IP application layer incorporates the session and presentation layers.

- The transport layer is comparable in each.
- The Internet layer (TCP/IP) and the network layer (OSI) are comparable.
- Both have packet switched technology.
- Networking professionals need to understand both models.

The differences can be summarised as follows:

- TCP/IP appears simpler because it has fewer layers.
- TCP/IP combines the presentation and session layers into the application layer.
- TCP/IP combines the seven-layer data link and physical layers into one layer, known as the network access layer.
- The OSI seven-layer model is used as a guide around which networks are built.

TCP/IP protocols are the standards around which the Internet was developed. These protocols are in use across the entire Internet, which gives the model great credibility.

> —————————— CRUCIAL TIP ——————————
> Take the time to learn these similarities and differences – it will be time well spent!

Quick test

Draw a diagram that compares the OSI seven-layer model with the TCP/IP model. Briefly identify the similarities and differences between the two models.

> —————————— CRUCIAL TIP——————————
> Try to remember the staple diet of a networking professional – cola and sausage pizza! What does cola come in? A tin! And we all know what not to do with sausage pizza – don't throw it away!

Section 4

End of chapter assessment

Questions

1. Identify the layers of the OSI seven-layer model and briefly describe each one.
2. Identify the layers of the TCP/IP model and briefly describe the function of each one.
3. Compare and contrast the OSI seven-layer model and the TCP/IP model.

Answers

1. In this kind of question the examiner is looking for two things:

- your knowledge of the layers;
- your understanding of what each layer does.

Using a phrase (perhaps 'please do not throw sausage pizza away'), you can construct a diagram showing the OSI seven-layer model. For that 'finishing touch', you can show you understand which are application-related layers and which are networking related. You can also impress by stating that the seven-layer model is used as a guide around which networks are built. Next you need to discuss each layer in turn, highlighting the services and functions in each layer. If you can remember some of the standards (for example, JPEG, GIFF, RTF, etc., in the presentation layer), mention them. Remember each layer (apart from application) provides a service to the layer above and utilises the services of the layer below (apart from the physical layer). For really high marks you could also discuss data encapsulation at layers 1–4 and the fact that it is a data stream at layer 5 (remember 'British Forces Postal Service').

2. Again, the examiner is looking for two things:
   • your knowledge of the layers;
   • your understanding of the functions of the layers.

   Again, use a phrase ('A TIN') to help you remember the layers and their sequence. Draw a diagram and, to impress, show the difference between the application-orientated layers and the network-orientated ones. You may further impress by stating that the TCP/IP model, unlike the OSI seven-layer model, is actually implemented – it is the one around which the Internet is built. Next a discussion of each layer and its functions is required. Remember to include that each layer provides services to the layer above. High marks will be assured by discussing data encapsulation in the model (using the same mnemonic 'British Forces Postal Service').

3. This time the examiner is looking for the differences between the two models. The starting point is to construct a diagram similar to Figure 4.4, which compares the two models. It is worth spending some time getting this diagram correct as it will almost completely answer this question! By using the word 'compare' the examiner is asking for the similarities and, by 'contrast', the differences. Section 3 provides a summarised list of the similarities and differences. Your answer should include these but in a more discursive way. Howlever, make sure you make them easy to find and mark! Don't forget the major difference is that the OSI model is just that – a model – whereas the Internet is built around the TCP/IP model.

Section 5

Further reading and research

Most comprehensive texts on networking will provide you with further reading on this topic.

See the *www.PhilipIrving.com* website for up-to-date further reading and support for this chapter.

Cisco Networking Academy Program (2001) *First Year Companion Guide* (2nd edn) Cisco Press. ISBN: 1 58713 025 4. Chapters 2, 5–7 and 10–15.

Hodson, P. (2002) *Local Area Networks* (4th edn) Continuum. ISBN: 0 82645 866 1. Chapter 7.

Chapter 5
Popular technologies

Chapter summary

A network has a physical shape (topology – see Chapter 3) and an implementation, a set of protocols and hardware (technology). Over the years a number of technologies have been established but, like most industries, the market has largely settled for just a few. This chapter doesn't seek to cover all the technologies but only those worthy of note:

- **Ethernet** – without doubt the most popular LAN technology in the world. Hugely dominant and likely to stay that way.
- **Token Ring** – a worthy alternative to Ethernet which is still around, although it is becoming less popular.
- **FDDI** – in early 2003, FDDI was still the standard for backbone cabling although everyone expects gigabit Ethernet to take over.
- **ATM** – this is important as it harmonises the telephone network with computer networking, providing the highest speed transfer of external data to the organisation. It has also been implemented inside organisations as a LAN backbone.

Learning outcomes

After studying this chapter you should aim to test your achievement of the following outcomes. You should be able to:

Outcome 1: Ethernet networks
Understand the development, variants, method of access, typical uses and hardware components of Ethernet networks. Question 1 at the end of this chapter will test your ability to do this.

Outcome 2: Token Ring networks
Understand the development, variants, method of access, typical uses and hardware components of Token Ring networks. Question 2 at the end of this chapter will test your ability to do this.

Outcome 3: FDDI networks
Understand the operation, typical uses and hardware components of fibre distributed data interface (FDDI) networks. Question 3 at the end of this chapter will test your ability to do this.

Outcome 4: ATM Networks
Understand the operation, typical uses and hardware components of asynchronous transmission mode (ATM) networks. Question 4 at the end of this chapter will test your ability to do this.

How will you be assessed on this?

The technologies covered in this chapter represent the range of technologies in use today. The assessment of your studies is almost guaranteed to include them. Commonly, assessments are in the form of a design (in an assignment) and, as part of a TCT, questions regarding their particular features. You are often asked to describe the method of access of either Ethernet of the Token Ring, or to discuss Ethernet and its variants.

Section 1

Ethernet networks

Ethernet (IEEE 802.3) networks are the most popular networks in the world, and the technology is continuing to develop in response to various organisations' needs. It is widely implemented everywhere and looks like being the LAN of choice for some considerable period of time. As such, it is the network that is given the greatest treatment in this chapter.

Method of access

Initially Ethernet was a bus network (see Chapter 3), and its method of access is known as Carrier Sense Multiple Access with Collision Detection (CSMA/CD). The assembled data is broadcast (like a TV programme) over the media. The steps involved in a transmission can be summarised as follows:

- Listen to network.
- If it is clear, begin transmission of the frame.
- Continue to listen to the network.
- If a collision is heard (two frames colliding with one another), send out a jamming signal.
- If the jamming signal is heard, stop transmitting and wait for a random time period before retrying.

Figure 5.1 shows two Ethernet stations (A and C) that wish to transmit at the same time. Both are listening to the network: there is no transmission and so both begin to transmit. The frames eventually collide and both are lost, requiring retransmission. The time taken from transmission to collision to the end of the random time period is, therefore, wasted time.

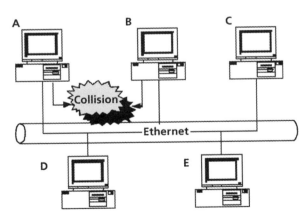

Figure 5.1   An Ethernet collision

The problem with traditional Ethernet (10Base2 and 10Base5) is that, the more frames that are transmitted, the higher is the probability of a collision. And the greater the number of collisions, the more frames that require retransmission. Whilst all this is going on, very little data is getting through, and the users experience severe delays. This tends to happen when the data presented to the network exceeds 7 Mbps. Traditional Ethernet is therefore useful in situations of moderate load and particularly useful for short, bursty traffic loads.

CRUCIAL TIP

'Load' can be affected by the number of computers *and* the amount of data they transmit.

CRUCIAL CONCEPT

It is very important to understand the way the medium is shared; indeed, this is absolutely fundamental when moving on to discuss other networks and other variants of Ethernet. An easy way to remember this is to draw an analogy. Suppose that an army commander needs to get a message through enemy territory during a battle. He writes a note and gives this to the first dispatcher. Both listen and, if all is calm, the dispatcher goes out. Once he's gone the commander listens again. If a shot is heard, the commander knows the message didn't get through and so sends out another dispatcher. The more intense the battle, the more chance there is of a 'collision'. And the more collisions, the longer it takes to get the message through.

Ethernet frame formats

Whatever the variant of Ethernet, they all use the same frame format. As discussed in Chapter 3, data needs to be broken into packets to be sent across the network. Packets are the units used by the Internet protocol (IP) structure (see Chapter 11). A particular technology uses a specific frame type. Ethernet frame type is shown in Figure 5.2. Being a CSMA/CD method of access, Ethernet requires a minimum frame size in order that errors can be detected properly. If the data to be sent makes the frame smaller than that minimum size, it needs to be 'padded out' (frame contents are discussed in more detail in Chapter 3).

8	6	6	2	0–1500	(46–0)	4
Preamble	Destination address	Source address	Length	Data	Padding	CRC

Figure 5.2 Ethernet frame structure

Ethernet variants

Ethernet is constantly being developed. Early Ethernet utilised a bus or tree topology, whereas later versions used a star topology. The naming convention (shown in Figure 5.3) has been adopted for Ethernet.

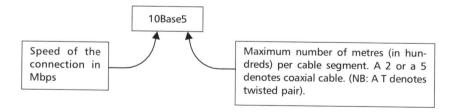

Figure 5.3 Ethernet naming convention

Table 5.1 summarises the variants.

Table 5.1   Ethernet variants

Name	Cable type	Max. dist. /segment (m)	Max. speed (Mbps)	Topology	Max. nodes per segment	Max. segments per LAN
10Base5	10 mm coaxial	500	10	bus/tree	100	5
10Base2	5 mm coaxial	185	10	bus/tree	30	5
10BaseT	twisted pair	100	10	star	2	n/a
100BaseT	twisted pair	100	100	star	2	n/a
1000BaseT (gigabit Ethernet)	twisted pair	100	1000	star	2	n/a

---

CRUCIAL TIP

Ethernet is the world's most popular networking technology and, as such, its importance can hardly be overlooked either in an exam or in the real world.

10Base5

This was the original Ethernet development. It is easily distinguished by the thick 10 mm coaxial cable on which it is based, and it operates on the bus/tree topology. Because of the great coverage length achieved for each segment of this cable, after initially being the standard it came to be used as the backbone connecting LANs formed with 10Base2 cabling. Cabling 10Base5 was difficult because of the thickness and rigidity of the cable used. Attaching this cable required the use of a specialist device, called a **tap** (see Figure 5.4). Figure 5.5 shows how a tap is installed. Other than this, only two network cards (with either in-built transceivers or external transceivers) and terminators were required. 10Base5 was expensive because of the costs associated with the cables and taps. However, current prices are not available as this variant of Ethernet is no longer used.

Figure 5.4   Combined 10Base5 Ethernet tap and transceiver (courtesy of Blackbox Networks).

The advantage of 10Base5 was the long length of cable run, which allowed the network to be extended to cover large buildings.

The disadvantages were the difficulties in laying the cable (due to its rigidity) and the costs of the cable, taps and transceivers.

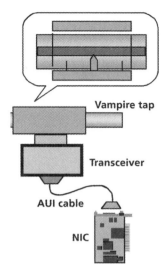

Figure 5.5   Installation of a tap (courtesy of Surasak Sanguanpong, Kasetsart University, Thailand)

10Base2

This was a very popular variant of Ethernet, mainly due to its very low installation and hardware costs (hence it was also known as 'Cheapernet'). 10Base2 is based on 5 mm coaxial cable (very similar to TV aerial cable) and, in the main British naval connectors (see Figure 5.6). Its price made it popular for use in classrooms and for small networking applications (e.g. lawyers' offices, estate agents, small companies and in the home). Adding machines to the network was also easy – all that was required was to disconnect the cable at the required point (when the network wasn't in use) and to connect the new computer. Providing certain standards were observed, the computer would operate. All that is needed to construct a two-station 10Base2 network are two 10Base2 Ethernet cards (NICs) (approximately £10 each at early 2003 prices), a piece of cable (around £5 at early 2003 prices) and two terminating resistors (50p at early 2003 prices) (Figure 5.6 also shows these components).

Figure 5.6   Typical 10Base5 connectors

The typical advantages of 10Base2 are:

- its low cost;
- ease of setup;
- the minimum kit requirements;
- the single cabling, which minimises disruption to the installation.

It typical disadvantages are:

- its poor performance for busy networks (e.g. college multimedia lab);
- cable breaks affect all computers.

CRUCIAL CONCEPT

10Base2 and 10Base5 are both based on differing versions of coaxial cable and represent the 'older' type of Ethernet. Most new installations use twisted pair cabling, as detailed below.

10BaseT

Whilst 10Base2 probably ensured the success of Ethernet as a technology, compared to its competitors it still suffered from cable break problems. Also, in the mid-1990s many organisations were looking to structure their communications and cabling, and Token Ring (its main competitor) was better suited to this. Hence 10BaseT Ethernet was developed.

10BaseT Ethernet is based upon a star technology with a device called a **hub** (see Figure 5.7) at the centre. 10BaseT uses RJ-45 connectors and twisted pair cabling (see Figure 5.8). This makes the system resilient to cable breaks and also makes it suitable for structured cabling. Thus the management and maintenance of the cabling are somewhat easier than in the past. The method of access is, however, no different. Inside the hub all the ports are connected together just as in a bus topology and so collisions occur and capacity is lost. The network therefore still works as though it were a bus topology.

Figure 5.7   10BaseT hub

The cabling, hubs and network cards for 10BaseT are competitively priced. At early 2003 prices a card will cost £10, a hub less than £20, a 100m drum of cable £25 and the connectors about 5p each. Thus a two-station network could be set up for about £50.

10BaseT was (and still is) popular for large organisations, such as universities, colleges, call centres, etc. It is also rapidly taking over from 10Base2 and, as such, is being used in most organisations (including the home). As structured cabling is recommended by the EIA and TIA for all new installations, this form of cabling is becoming very popular.

Figure 5.8   Twisted pair cabling and an RJ-45 connector (courtesy of Cisco Systems Inc.)

The advantages of 10BaseT are:

- its structured cabling;
- its resilience to cable breaks;
- the low cost of its components;
- company reorganisation is easier to accomplish.

Its disadvantages are:

- capacity is still lost to collisions;
- the installation costs are high compared to 10Base2 but cheaper than other structured cabling;
- the hub represents a single point of failure (as with all star-based technologies).

100BaseT

100BaseT was a major breakthrough in Ethernet technology. Whilst still a star-based topology and whilst still using the same connectors and cabling, the hub used in 10BaseT was replaced with either a 100BaseT hub or a 100BaseT switch. Both provide a possible 100 Mbps throughput but the hub is still subject to the collisions found with the 10BaseT Ethernet. Through the use of the switch, the ports are no longer connected together internally but, instead, the connections between the ports are 'switched' together as and when necessary for data transfer (see Figure 5.9). This means collisions are virtually eliminated as only two devices are switched together at any one time. This allows for a far greater throughput to be realised. Most 100BaseT networks use switches because of their increased throughput – a full duplex switch will allow the connected NICs to realise 100 Mbps data transfer, inbound and outbound simultaneously.

The switches also allow simultaneous 100 Mbps transfers between many pairs of ports, thus increasing substantially the throughput of the network and firmly establishing Ethernet as the network of choice for most organisations. Although 100BaseT still uses the CSMA/CD method of access, collisions are not a problem. Further, 100BaseT is available in full duplex, using two pairs of twisted pair – one for transmit and one for receive. This gives 100 Mbps send and simultaneous 100 Mbps receive.

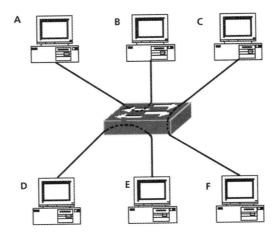

Figure 5.9   Switched ports

The costs of 100BaseT were initially high but, as with most computer products, their acceptance by the market has caused prices to tumble. Switches can be bought from as little as £30 (at early 2003 prices).

The major advantages of 100BaseT are:

- the virtual elimination of collisions;
- the high-speed data throughput;
- it is the quickest desktop networking solution;
- its costs are now very low, making it the obvious choice.

The main disadvantage of 100BaseT is the switch, which represents a single point of failure (as with all star-based technologies).

——————————— CRUCIAL CONCEPT ———————————

In early 2003, 100BaseT was the EIA/TIA's recommended desktop networking standard.

1000BaseT (or Gigabit Ethernet)

Following the successful development of 100BaseT (which took only 18 months), the Ethernet Alliance rushed to develop the next generation. Unfortunately, this took a lot longer than 18 months, but Gigabit Ethernet was finally launched at the end of the 1990s. Using the existing cabling (category 5) and the same frame format, Gigabit Ethernet is an easy upgrade path for 100BaseT users. Gigabit Ethernet will be found on servers and in the networking infrastructure that provides connections between switches. However, there is a the possibility of 1000 Mbps available at the desktop.

As Gigabit Ethernet is becoming adopted more widely its prices are continuing to fall. Typically, cards cost around £105 (at early 2003 prices). Again, like 100BaseT, Gigabit Ethernet provides both full and half-duplex operation, offering the possibility of simultaneous 1000 Mbps receive and transmit.

The major advantage of 1000BaseT is its very fast connection speeds. Its major disadvantage is the switch, which represents a single point of failure (as with all star-based technologies).

Wireless LAN (WLAN)

WLANs are an alternative to conventional wired networks. Many new products have been developed utilising this network and, recently many organisations (in particular, hotels and airports) are making use of them. WLANs offer a very flexible alternative to wired networks as they employ radio waves as the medium of transmission rather than copper or fibre cabling (Figure 5.10). WLANs operate in much the same way as the conventional Ethernet (on a CSMA/CD basis) but they provide less bandwidth than conventional wired systems. Typically, WLANs provide 11 Mbps shared across a total of eight devices, as opposed to 100 Mbps per device which is the norm in wired networks. There is a faster WLAN at 55 Mbps but the frequency at which it operates was not legal in a number of countries in early 2003.

The setup of WLANs is very simple. An access point (essentially a radio transceiver) is needed that connects to the network. This connection is usually a UTP connection and commonly supplies power to the transceiver as well as connection to the organisational LAN. The transceiver usually has eight channels that facilitate the connection of eight networking devices per access point. Each PC, laptop or PDA connecting to the WLAN needs a WLAN card and must be registered as being able to use the WLAN. After that, all is ready to go.

The normal rules governing radio transmission apply, that is – the closer to the access point, the stronger the signal and the better the speed of connection. At the fringes of radio coverage, the signal becomes weak and speed suffers. The placement of access points is also crucial – these must be at a sufficient distance apart so as not to interfere with each other's channels.

In early 2003, a WLAN starter pack (consisting of three WLAN cards and an access point) cost £450. Although this is far more expensive than conventional wired LANs, it requires fewer cables – which means less disruption and lower installation costs.

Figure 5.10   Typical WLAN implementation

The major advantages of WLANs are:

- they are an easy, low-cost installation;
- they provide connection unobtrusively (e.g. to airline lounges);
- they can be deployed rapidly;
- their mobility.

The major disadvantages of WLANs are:

- their slow speed;
- security issues (although these can be addressed, there is still a danger of eaves-dropping);
- the increased radio waves in the working environment and the associated health worries.

Quick test

Briefly list the main variants of Ethernet, together with their advantages and disadvantages.

Section 2

Token Ring (IEEE 802.5)

Token Ring was developed by IBM and accepted by the International Standards Organisation and the IEEE. It was a popular alternative to Ethernet, particularly with companies who needed a guaranteed response time from their network. Unfortunately, Token Ring never became as cheap as Ethernet and, so, never became as popular. At one point, Token Ring was far faster than Ethernet with its 16 Mbps version (compared with Ethernet's 10 Mbps). Token Ring's method of access is also much fairer, which means it is able to use the whole bandwidth.

Token Ring has been included in this chapter to show there are alternatives to Ethernet. You may well also meet Token Ring in your future employment.

Method of access and operation

As Token Ring is based upon a ring technology (see Figure 5.11), the best place to start is with its method of access. A data frame (called the 'free token') circulates continually, passing through each machine on the network. When a machine (e.g. A) wishes to transmit data, it waits for the free token to pass through its interface. When a free token passes its interface, it sets the free token bit to indicate that this frame is now busy. It then inserts its data (including the source and destination address) into the frame. This data frame then circulates around the network until it reaches the destination machine (e.g. C). The destination machine copies the data and sets flags (in the frame) to say that the address was recognised and the data copied. The frame continues to circulate until it reaches the sender. When the sender receives the frame, it checks to see if the address has been recognised and if the data has been copied. If not, the frame continues to circulate. If the flags were set, the sender removes the data and resets the token to indicate that the frame is free once again.

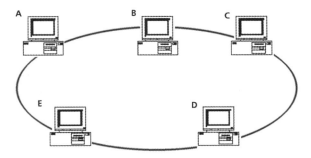

Figure 5.11   Token Ring

However, there are possible problems with this system. For example, what happens if the destination machine either doesn't exist (or goes down), or the sender goes down before the frame is cleared? In the former case, the data packet would circulate several times, but eventually, the sender would give up after several attempts and remove the frame. The latter case is more serious – Token Ring protocols require the sender to remove the data from the frame. If the sender goes down, the data will not be removed and the frame would circulate endlessly. There would be no free token and no other machine could access the network. Enter the monitor station. The monitor station, as its name suggests, monitors the frames sent round the network. When the network starts up, all the machines make a bid to be the monitor station, and protocols determine which machine will be the monitor station and the rest go on standby.

As a frame passes through the monitor station, the station sets the monitor bit in the frame to 1. Should the monitor station detect a frame with its monitor bit already set to 1, it knows the frame has traversed the entire ring once and therefore now seems to be circulating endlessly. The monitor station can then take action to clean up the network by replacing the frame with a free token frame. Supposing machine B is the monitor station, we will re-run the example above. Machine A transmits the data packet to machine C. The frame passes through machine B (the monitor station), which sets the monitor bit. The frame passes through machine C which copies the data. Machine C then sets the address recognised bit and the data copied bit. The frame then passes through machines D and E. Let's assume the sender (=machine A) has suffered a failure and has gone down. The switching technology in Token Ring means machine A will be bypassed and so the frame passes to machine B. At this point, the frame is circulating endlessly and so no one else can transmit. The monitor station (machine B) notices that the monitor bit is already set, indicating it has seen the frame before. The monitor station generates a new free token and places it on to the network (in place of the data packet). As a further precaution, the machines 'on standby' to become monitor stations periodically inquire whether they can become the monitor station. Thus, if the monitor station should go down, the network will be able to continue.

CRUCIAL TIP

An analogy to help you remember Token Ring operation is a relay race – you can't run without the batten (the free token) and you must pass it on when you have run round the track once. The batten gives you access to the track (the media).

Token Ring hardware

Although a ring, Token Ring operates as a star format and has, at its centre a multistation access unit or (MAU) (see Figure 5.12). The MAU simply connects the stations together in a ring but, in the event of a cable being broken or a machine going down, the MAU can bypass the port. MAUs cost around £500 for 16 ports (early 2003 prices). Every machine on the network needs a Token Ring networking card which, at early 2003 prices, were about £40. The cable used for a Token Ring is, typically, shielded twisted pair (STP) (see Chapter 3).

Figure 5.12   Token Ring MAU (courtesy of Blackbox Networks)

Token Ring frame structure

Token Ring has two frame formats – a free token frame and a data frame. Figure 5.13 shows the free token and Figure 5.14 the data frame.

Start delimeter (1 byte)	Access control (1 byte)	End delimeter (1 byte)

Figure 5.13   Structure of Token Ring free token

Start delimeter (1 byte)	Access control (1 byte)	Destination address (2–6 bytes)	Source address (2–6 bytes)	Length (2 bytes)	Date (no minimum size)	CRC (4 bytes)	End delimeter	Status flags (address recognised, frame copied, etc.) (1 byte)

Figure 5.14   Structure of Token Ring data frame

Unlike Ethernet, there is no minimum data size for a Token Ring frame. The monitor bits etc., are found in the access control part of the frame (Figure 5.15). The operation of Token Ring lies in the detail behind this bit. A free token is set to 0 bits but, when claimed, it is set to 1 bit. Similarly, the monitor bit has a value of 1 when set. As Figure 5.15 suggests, Token Ring allows for priorities to be set. When it is waiting to transmit, if a station receives a busy token it can place its assigned priority number into the reservation field. When the machine currently holding the free token releases it, the reservation field is moved to the priority field. Thus only the bidder (or one with higher priority) is able to claim this 'priority token'. This allows for the support of stations with priority traffic (e.g. real-time data for robot control or applications with synchronous data flows of (low-rate) video).

Access Control			
Priority bits (3)	Token bit (1)	Monitor bit (1)	Reservation bits (3)

Figure 5.15   Structure of the access control part of the data frame

Advantages/disadvantages of Token Ring

Token Ring has the following advantages:

- It is a much fairer method of access.
- Bandwidth is not lost to collisions.
- Performance is more predictable (adding an extra machine will slow the network down proportionately).

- Speed (compared with standard 10Base5 and 10Base2 Ethernet).
- Signal quality is greater as each machine regenerates the signal. Token Ring networks, therefore, can span a greater distance.
- It is able to prioritise data flows.

Its disadvantages are as follows:

- Costs are much higher than Ethernet.
- Speed is not as great as 100BaseT.

Quick test

Briefly describe the mode of operation of a Token Ring network.

CRUCIAL TIP

Token Ring and Ethernet are two of the most popular technologies ever. In an exam you are sometimes asked to compare and contrast these technologies.

Section 3

Fibre-Distributed Data Interface (FDDI)

At the moment (2003), FDDI is still the recommended networking backbone standard, although this might change with the introduction of Gigabit Ethernet. However, as it has been the backbone standard for some time, there are a large number of installations that employ FDDI.

Method of access and operation

FDDI operates in a similar manner to Token Ring and it is also based on a ring topology. It uses fibre optic cabling (see Figure 5.16) and offers speeds of up to 100 Mbps in private networks. Its dual concentric rings also provide greater resilience to cable breaks (if one cable is cut or breaks, the data can use the other cable). One of the rings operates in a clockwise fashion and the other anti-clockwise to ensure all nodes are in reach. FDDI uses the same method of operation and access to the media as Token Ring networks and it uses similar flags for address recognised and data copied. FDDI is used in backbone cabling and to link together networking devices, such as switches and hubs (see Chapter 6), as shown in Figure 5.17.

Figure 5.16   Fibre optic cabling (courtesy of Cisco Systems Inc.)

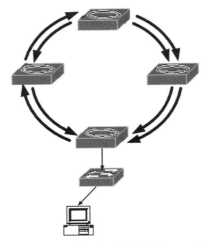

Figure 5.17   A typical FDDI deployment

FDDI hardware

As FDDI is deployed as a backbone, the networking devices commonly have in-built FDDI support and they link directly to concentrators which then connect to the ring. In early 2003, concentrators were almost impossible to buy and, when they were available, were prohibitively expensive at £55 000. They also require fibre optic cabling.

Advantages/disadvantages of FDDI

The major advantages of FDDI are as follows:

- Its speed as compared with such technologies as conventional Ethernet and Token Ring (FDDI was available when 10Base2 was the standard for LAN cabling).
- Its robustness.
- The distance it can cover – fibre optic can carry data further than copper without the need for signal regeneration (2 km between nodes).
- Its resistance to interference (fibre optic is virtually immune to interference from outside sources – see Chapter 3).
- Its suitability for interconnecting buildings. (Copper is dangerous as it could be struck by lightning and conduct the current).

The major disadvantages of FDDI are as follows:

- Its speed when compared to Gigabit Ethernet.
- It is not in harmony with the telephone network and therefore slower over public networks.

—————— CRUCIAL CONCEPT ——————

For organisations wanting a high-speed, interference-free backbone, FDDI was the technology of choice. In early 2003 it was still the recommended backbone standard.

Quick test

Briefly describe an FDDI network and its uses.

Section 4

Asynchronous Transmission Method (ATM)

Introduction

The telecommunications standards of the late 1990s were primarily designed to carry the voice. This was a time when computers were less powerful and slower than today. The design criteria for these networks specified reliability rather than speed and, hence, the criteria included error-checking facilities. The computing world is now very different, and ATM was devised as part of a review of telecommunications. ATM operates in harmony with the telecommunications network and provides organisations with a high-speed link to the outside world. As it is half as fast again as FDDI, it is also used as a backbone inside organisations.

ATM

As has just been noted, ATM was a breakthrough in communications technology. When used as a network backbone, ATM provides 155 Mbps transfer speed – higher than any available before. However, that was only the beginning. ATM was originally developed for public broadband networks but became the technology of choice for private networks and LANs. ATM is a packet-switching multiplexing transmission technique that makes use of fixed-length packets (called **cells**). Based around switches (called **cellplexes**) like FDDI, the cellplexes identify the cells' destinations and then forwards them. This means that ATM responds reasonably well to demands but, and more importantly, it can handle any type of content – cells could also be data, video, audio or speech. Just as network interface cards are a standard part of in the ISO seven-layer model, ATM is a standard in the digital telecommunications protocol. Because of this, it is able to work internally and externally at 155 Mbps. This speed was a major breakthrough: the best external data rate available in the UK jumped from 2 Mbps to 155 Mbps. Figure 5.18 shows a typical ATM implementation. Many high-end server manufacturers (e.g. Sun Microsystems) manufactured servers with in-built ATM support.

ATM cellplex

Switch with inbuilt ATM

Server with ATM NIC

Figure 5.18 A typical ATM configuration

Advantages/disadvantages of ATM

ATM has the following advantages:

- It is harmonised with the telephone network, providing 155 Mbps connection external to the organisation.
- It has a higher speed than FDDI.

The disadvantages of ATM include the following:

- Costs (compared with the gigabit Ethernet).
- Speed (compared with the gigabit Ethernet).

CRUCIAL CONCEPT

ATM is truly revolutionary, representing the harmonisation of the telephone and data networks. As an international standard, ATM paves the way for high-speed international data links. However, although sometimes still implemented as a backbone, at 155 Mbps ATM is rapidly losing ground to Gigabit Ethernet.

Quick test

Briefly describe an ATM network and outline why it is so revolutionary.

Section 5

End of chapter assessment

Questions

1. Discuss the mode of access of Ethernet technology, and outline the major developments of this technology.
2. Discuss the way Token Ring operates. Highlight its advantages and disadvantages compared to conventional (10Base2 and 10Base5) Ethernet.
3. Discuss FDDI technology, highlighting its mode of operation and typical uses.
4. Discuss ATM technology, explaining why ATM is so revolutionary.

Answers

1. This question in one form or another is very popular in assessments and exams. Such is the importance of the technology that the examiner is almost obliged to test you on it! What the examiner is essentially looking for is that you:

- understand the method of accessing the media (CSMA/CD);
- understand that it is unfair and can result in a large amount of wasted bandwidth;
- can sensibly discuss its shortcomings.

Once you have demonstrated this you should aim to discuss each variant within the technology. For each you should discuss:

- its topology and typical configuration;
- the speeds attainable;

- the distances covered and typical costs;
- typical connectors and wiring;
- typical applications;
- advantages and disadvantages.

You should then summarise your answer, drawing conclusions relevant to the question.

2. To answer this you need to highlight the way in which Token Ring technology operates and draw out the fact that it is a much fairer method of access than CSMA/CD. You should outline the typical structure of Token Ring, its topology and typical applications. It is important that you highlight that the expected delay for Token Ring is proportional to the number of stations connected. You should next compare and contrast Token Ring with Ethernet and highlight the relevant advantages and disadvantages of each. In doing this you will need to discuss each one with respect to the various stages of Ethernet development.

3. To answer this question you will need to highlight the mode of operation of Token Ring networks and the fact that FDDI is essentially the same. You should outline the topology and typical cabling solutions of the network and ideally show these diagrammatically. You should also outline the speeds attainable by FDDI and its typical applications. It is worth pointing out that fibre covers a longer distance than copper and is less susceptible to noise and errors than copper. Also highlight the fact that FDDI was the EIA/TIA recommended backbone for many years.

4. To answer this you will need to discuss ATM technology. In particular, the assessor is looking for your ability to discuss what is so radical about this technology and the major breakthrough it represents. Don't disappoint – demonstrate you know it is internationally agreed standard in harmony with the telephone network. You should also mention that it was used by organisations for a number of years as a backbone as it was faster than FDDI technology. However, you should note that take-up was not tremendous as Gigabit technology was on the horizon. You must make sure you mention that ATM is in harmony with the telecommunications network and that it can be provide high-speed links externally to the organisation.

Section 6

Further reading and research

See the *www.Philiplrving.com* website for up-to-date further reading and support for this chapter.

Cisco Networking Academy Program (2001) *First Year Companion Guide* (2nd edn). Cisco Press. ISBN: 1 58713 025 4. Chapters 5 and 7.

Hodson, P. (2002) *Local Area Networks* (4th edn). Continuum. ISBN: 0 82645 866 1. Chapters 9 and 10.

www.bt.com (you can find the prices for external lines from here – e.g. ATM) (accessed July 2003)

http://www.gigabit-Ethernet.org/ (The Gigabit Ethernet Alliance) (accessed July 2003)

Chapter 6
Popular networking devices

Chapter summary

The purpose of a network is to interconnect computers to facilitate the transfer of data. To achieve this, a number of networking devices are available. The principal ones are:

- NICs
- modem
- repeater
- hub
- bridge
- switch
- MAU
- router
- gateway.

Each is explored in turn in this chapter.

Learning outcomes

After studying this chapter you should aim to test your achievement of the following outcomes. You should be able to:

Outcome 1: Interconnection provided by a network interface card (NIC)
Understand what a NIC is and its essential role in networking.

Outcome 2: Collision and broadcast domains
Understand what is meant by the terms collision and broadcast domain and understand which devices provide containment.

Outcome 3: Interconnection based on a repeater
Understand the function, interconnections and typical uses of a repeater.

Outcome 4: Interconnection based on a hub
Understand the function, interconnections and typical uses of a hub.

Outcome 5: Interconnection based on a bridge
Understand the function, interconnections and typical uses of a bridge.

Outcome 6: Interconnection based on a switch
Understand the function, interconnections and typical uses of a switch.

Outcome 7: Interconnection based on a MAU
Understand the function, interconnections and typical uses of a MAU.

Outcome 8: Interconnection based on a router
Understand the function, interconnections and typical uses of a router.

Outcome 9: Interconnection based around a gateway
Understand the need for a gateway and its role in internetworking.

How will you be assessed on this?

Understanding the function of networking devices is usually assessed in one of two ways: either directly in an examination or TCT question or indirectly through a design-type assignment. A typical TCT question is given at the end of this chapter.

Section 1

Interconnection provided by a Network Interface Card (NIC)

Introduction

NICs are a crucial part of networking, allowing the computer to be connected to the network.

CRUCIAL TIP

You may recall that, in Chapter 3, we compared networking to plumbing. We will again use this analogy as networking interconnecting devices can often be described more easily this way.

An NIC is a printed circuit board that goes inside a host computer (known as a **host**) to provide it with LAN connectivity. NICs fit into a PC's expansion slot (Figure 6.1 shows three NICs, the oldest being from the 1980s and the smallest from 1998). NICs are also known as **network adaptors**. They are manufactured to operate with a particular networking technology and particular variants of that technology. For example, a 10Base2 networking card is usually different from a 10BaseT networking card because of the difference in the cabling.

Figure 6.1   Typical network interface cards

In laptop computers, NICs are usually PCMCIA devices. Such is the popularity of Ethernet that some computers even come with ethernet NICs built in.

The NIC's function is to connect the host to the network media, and it is the basic hardware component of network communications. The NIC translates the parallel signals produced by the computer into serial signals suitable for transmission across the network. The binary 1s or 0s are usually turned into electrical pulses or, sometimes, into light or radio waves suitable for transmission over the medium. To make this transmission, the NIC needs a transceiver unit. Most NICs for Ethernet (except 10Base5) have this built in.

NICs are layer two devices in the OSI seven-layer model as they work on frames and have media access control capabilities – including (in the case of Ethernet) an address that is unique in the world. This address is a 48-bit number (usually expressed in hexadecimal). The first 24 bits are a vendor ID and the second 24 a vendor-assigned unique serial number within that ID.

It is important to consider the computer's architecture when selecting an NIC, for two reasons. First, the NIC must match the host computer's architecture. For example, an ISA will not connect to a PCI-only architecture. Secondly the architecture should be capable of supporting the NIC's speed requirements. For example, a 100BaseT ISA network card could never achieve more than 8 Mbps as that is the speed limit of the ISA architecture. Other important factors to consider when selecting an NIC are:

- the operating system (are the NIC drivers supported?);
- the media type (UTP, coaxial);
- the network architecture;
- the data transfer speed.

CRUCIAL TIP

In plumbing terms, the NIC is the equivalent of the water inlet/waste outlet on a washing machine. The water inlet gives the washing machine access to the services of the water network. The drains then provide services for output.

Quick test

Briefly outline the function of an NIC and the factors that should influence their choice.

Section 2

Collision and broadcast domains

Introduction

There are two major considerations when discussing a networking kit based upon Ethernet technology. As we saw in Chapter 5, Ethernet method of access (CSMA/CD) causes collisions, which can be a major problem as these waste bandwidth and can cause delays. There is also the possibility of broadcasting a transmission to all the stations on the network. It is essential you appreciate these considerations before looking at networking hardware in more detail.

Broadcast domain

As noted above, it is often necessary to send a message to every machine on a network. System administrators often need to alert all users about a problem, an impending shutdown, etc. To broadcast, the broadcast address (all the 1s in Ethernet) is placed into the destination address field of the frame. Every machine on the network will then receive this frame. If a great many machines send out broadcasts at once, this places an unnecessarily heavy load on the LAN. Ideally, the number of machines which receive this broadcast should be limited or they should be grouped together in some way. Such groupings are termed **broadcast domains**. A networking kit is available to contain such broadcasts – the router (see later).

CRUCIAL TIP

Think of a large company with several departments. The sales director may send out a sales update to his or her staff, as might the production manager. However, those people won't send the updates to other departments in the company as this would be unnecessary. They are thus broadcasting the information to their own departments but departmental structure ensures the information broadcast is contained within the one department – broadcast containment. The departmental structure has split the company into broadcast domains.

Collision domain

As we saw in Chapter 5, Ethernet relies on collision detection to operate and, the busier the network, the more collisions. The more collisions, the more capacity is wasted. Thus it is necessary to control the number of collisions to make better use of the available capacity. Given the unrestricted access stations have when transmitting on Ethernet, the only way to control collisions is to limit the number of stations on a network without reducing connectivity. The solution to this problem is to divide the network up to establish collision domains that will contain the collisions. Again, networking kit is available that contains collisions – bridges, switches and routers (see later).

CRUCIAL TIP

Imagine there was only one road to serve an entire country. Every car journey made involved using that road. Also imagine there were few regulations governing access to that road – a quick look and on you go! Obviously, there would be a great number of accidents (collisions). One solution would be to provide local roads for local traffic, thus reducing the number of collisions on that main road. Hence collision domains would have been created to prevent unnecessary traffic from entering the main road. Junctions would join the roads providing access but fewer collisions.

The terms 'broadcast' and 'collision domains' will become clearer as we explore each piece of hardware in turn.

Quick test

Briefly discuss what is meant by the terms 'broadcast domain' and 'collision domain'.

Section 3

Interconnection based on a repeater

Introduction

Repeaters are an essential part of ethernet technology as they provide a means by which the length of a cable run can be extended. As we saw in Chapter 5, there are limits to the length of cabling used on Ethernet and these restrictions can often pose problems. Repeaters help to overcome these. There are three types of repeaters – coaxial repeaters, UTP repeaters and repeaters that convert between UTP and coaxial cable.

As an ethernet signal nears the end of its cable run or gets close to the maximum number of nodes per segment the technology can handle, it becomes weak – timing signals move out and the signal can become distorted. A repeater restores the signal to its original state and passes it on. To do this, the repeater must regenerate rather than amplify the signal (amplification would amplify the distortion and wouldn't address the timing issues). Thus a signal is received on one port of the repeater, is regenerated and then re-timed before being transmitted on the other ports. Repeaters are bidirectional devices that regenerate at the bit level. As such they are layer one networking devices. As they need to listen to a bit before regenerating it, they introduce a delay into the network of at least 1 bit. Repeaters have no effect on collision or broadcast domains.

Co-axial repeaters

As their name suggests, coaxial repeaters are used in 10Base2 and 10Base5 networks but there are strict limits to their use. For example, in a 10Base2 network, all that is allowed between the sender and the receiver are:

- a maximum of five segments (of which two must be free from nodes);
- a maximum of four repeaters;
- a maximum of three active segments;
- two transit segments.

(Alternatively, it is possible to have two active segments and three transit segments.)

CRUCIAL TIP
This limitation is often known as the 5-4-3-2 rule.

A segment ends when 30 nodes or 185 m are reached. At that point the signal is too weak to continue and needs to be repeated. Figure 6.2 shows a typical 10Base2 layout using a repeater. Figure 6.3 shows the limit between a sender and a receiver in a 10Base2 network – five segments (two empty) and four repeaters. This rule obviously limits the extent to which the network might grow but can be overcome by good design. By using a segment(s) as a backbone and by using multi-port repeaters, it is possible to design a network with more segments than this which still conforms to the 5-4-3-2 rule. In Figure 6.4 there are numerous segments but, between the nodes there are never more than five. For example, between points A and B there are only three segments (including segments A and B).

Figure 6.2   Two ethernet segments connected by repeaters

Figure 6.3   A typical 10Base2 network using repeaters

Figure 6.4   A well designed 10Base2 network with many segments
which still conforms to the 5-4-3-2 rule

UTP repeaters

UTP has even more restrictions than coaxial cabling:

- It can only have two nodes per segment.
- A segment can only be 100 m long.

These restrictions are a result of the 10BaseT ethernet being a star topology and because interconnection is carried out in the hub. However, there are occasions when a machine might need to be placed more than 100 m away from the hub. On such occasions a repeater can be used to extend the distance (to a maximum of 100 m either side of the repeater). Figure 6.5 shows a typical repeater implementation.

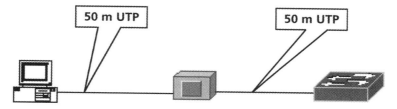

Figure 6.5   A typical UTP network with a repeater

UTP/coaxial converting repeater

As we saw in Chapter 5, all ethernet variants have the same frame format. Occasionally, however, there might be a need to connect machines (or even small LANs) that use coaxial cable to a network based on UTP and, rarely, vice versa. To achieve this, a coaxial-to-UTP repeater is used, as shown in Figure 6.6. Coaxial-to-UTP repeaters function in exactly the same way as other types of repeater. Their physical limitations depend on the media to which they are attached. As most installations now use UTP, these devices have become less common.

Figure 6.6   UTP-to-coaxial repeater

> ── CRUCIAL TIP ──
>
> Conversions cannot be made between Token Ring and Ethernet using such devices. Token Ring has a completely different frame structure and method of accessing the network. However, Token Ring cards can also function as repeaters!

Quick test

Briefly discuss the role of a repeater in a network.

Section 4

Interconnection based on a hub

Introduction

Hubs are part of ethernet technology where they connect devices together. Basically, there are three types of hubs: those used to connect coaxial cables, those that connect to UTP cabling and those used to cross media (e.g. UTP to coaxial). Although the media differ, essentially the hubs perform the same function. Hubs are layer-one devices of the OSI seven-layer model. They have little or no intelligence (as standard) and, basically they simply pass the data out across a number of ports. Hubs have no effect on collision or broadcast domains. UTP are the more commonly used hubs.

Coaxial hubs

Coaxial hubs have become almost redundant. They were used to connect multiple bus networks together to form a tree network (see Chapter 3). Technically, these hubs were multi-port repeaters. They took a coaxial cable and split it into many branches to form a tree network (with the original as the root) (Figure 6.7). As with a standard repeater, the signal out of each port was regenerated.

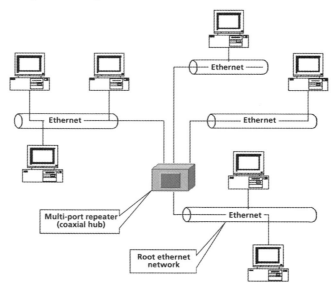

Figure 6.7 Ethernet network with a multi-port repeater

UTP hubs

These are by far the most common, forming the centre of a 10BaseT star network (see Chapter 3). The hub transforms the star typology into a logical bus network (see Figure 6.8): Whilst Ethernet network is a star topology, because it is 10BaseT it operates as a logical bus. Thus when one machine sends data to another machine, the data is received on port 1 of the hub but transmitted on all ports of the hub rather than just the port that the receiver is connected to. For this reason UTP hubs are sometimes called multi-port repeaters. As a signal is received, hubs regenerate and re-time the signal before sending it out on all the other ports. This is known as **concentration** and, sometimes, hubs are referred to as **concentrators**. Such regeneration and re-timing are carried out at the bit level, which means that hubs operate at level one of the OSI seven-layer model.

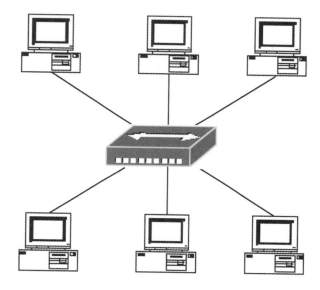

Figure 6.8   UTP hub

Essentially a hub:

- is used as a network concentration point;
- regenerates and re-times signals;
- cannot filter network traffic;
- cannot determine the best path for data;
- propagates signals across the network.

Hubs are most commonly used in 10BaseT networks but there are some that operate at 100 Mbps. These work in a similar manner to 10BaseT hubs but simply at a higher speed. To realise the full potential of 100BaseT, organisations should use switches at the centre of the star in 100BaseT networks (see Section 6 of this chapter).

─────────── CRUCIAL CONCEPT ───────────

Networking devices are specific to a technology and a topology.

Figure 6.9 shows the typical installation of 24-port 10BaseT hub. In large installations such as this, the hubs are themselves connected together.

Figure 6.9   10BaseT hub

Quick test

Briefly discuss the role of a hub in networking. Your answer should cover 10BaseT in particular.

Section 5

Interconnection based on a bridge

Introduction

Bridges are an essential piece of networking hardware. They enable traffic control and standards conversion and provide the essential connectivity. As we saw in Chapter 5, network technologies are incompatible, but bridges provide the means by which they can be joined. As also noted earlier, the maximum number of segments in Ethernet technology is five. Bridges, however, provide the means of extending them. Bridges also provide collision containment (discussed earlier in this Chapter) Bridges operate in layer two of the OSI seven-layer model. Being layer-two devices, they work at the data-frame level and are able to understand and forward frames. Bridges can be divided into two categories – those that perform technology conversions and those that work within a specific technology.

Technology conversion bridges

Often, data on a network needs to be available to machines that use different technologies. for example, a production department might use Token Ring technology but the sales department uses Ethernet. Emails and data, however, must be available to the whole company, irrespective of the technology. As bridges are intelligent devices and can see a frame in its entirety, they are able to extract the data from one frame and place it in another. In the above example, the bridge would take an Ethernet frame (from the sales department), extract the data and place it into a Token Ring frame before forwarding it on to the production network. (see Figure 6.10).

Figure 6.10   Bridging between Ethernet and Token Ring

Single technology bridges

Single technology bridges are the most common. They are used for one of two purposes – to:

- extend a technology (e.g. 10Base2) when its maximum length or number of nodes have been reached;
- perform traffic management by containing collisions and by preventing unnecessary traffic from crossing to the other side of the bridge.

10Base2 was useful in the early days of LANs when, for example, colleges and universities, had one LAN per classroom.When such organisations wanted to join their networks together, the limitations of 10Base2 became a problem (see Chapter 5). To extend their networks, a single technology bridge was used that divided the connected networks into distinct LANs.

The most common use of bridges today is, perhaps, for collision containment and traffic management. As bridges are intelligent devices, they can prevent frames passing through unless they are bound for a computer on the other side of the bridge. In Figure 6.11, a bridge has been installed in the middle of a busy network. The network designer has made sure the servers and the machines they serve are on the same side of the bridge. This means the bridge will quickly learn the MAC addresses of the connected machines and also which side they are on. Once it learns the addresses it will prevent frames from passing through the bridge unless they are bound for a machine on the other side. All things being equal, the effect will be to split the load on the network evenly – if the load was 6 Mbps before the bridge, it will be 3 Mbps (per segment) after installation of the bridge. The bridge will also half the number of collisions, thus breaking the network into two collision domains.

Figure 6.11   Bridged 10Base2

Quick test

Identify the two types of bridge and discuss briefly the situations in which they would be used.

Section 6

Interconnection based on a switch

Introduction

Switches are used at the centre of 100BaseT networks (as hubs were used at the centre of 10BaseT networks before 100BaseT came on to the market). As 100BaseT are currently the recommended standard for new desktop points, their importance cannot be emphasised enough.

Switches/switching

Switches can best be thought of as a combination of a bridge and a hub. As a layer-two device, a switch can read Ethernet frames and can make forwarding decisions according to the address (unlike a hub, which makes no decisions at all). Figure 6.12 shows the implementation of a switch. If machine A wished to transmit to machine D, in a hub environment the frame would be broadcast out of each port and would be heard by all the machines. The switch, just like a bridge, would know the MAC address of machine D and would know the port it was connected to. The switch would then send the frame *on that port only.*

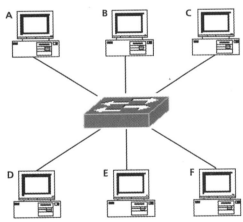

Figure 6.12 Implementation of a switch in a network

The effect of deploying a switch is to make the network more efficient and to increase throughput. Because the data is sent out on one port only, the number of collisions is reduced dramatically and bandwidth is available for other machines connected to the switch. Many pairs of machines can also communicate through the switch simultaneously at the network's full transmission speed. Thus in Figure 6.12 it would be possible for machines A and D, B and E and C and F to communicate simultaneously, each at the full bandwidth (see Figure 6.13). As the switch switches the two communicating ports together, it is only possible for these two machines to cause a collision, which greatly reduces the chances of a collision occurring. The switch thus creates multiple collision domains and this function is sometimes referred to as **micro-segmentation**.

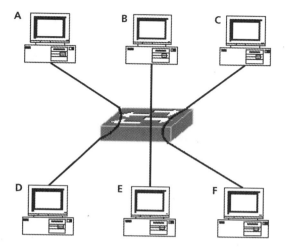

Figure 6.13   Ports being switched together

More expensive switches operate in full duplex (see Chapter 3) mode, which means they provide each host simultaneously with 100 Mbps transmission and 100 Mbps receive. To use this facility, the NIC must also be full duplex. Most switches are able to accommodate 10BaseT networking cards that operate at a slower speed (known as **asymmetric** switches). Those that are 100BaseT only are known as **symmetric** switches.

Quick test

Briefly outline the function of a switch and compare it with a hub.

Interconnection based on a MAU

Introduction

MAUs form the centre of a Token Ring network and, essentially, have the same function as a switch. Token ring technology is rarely installed nowadays, and it is often cheaper to replace an entire installation with 100BaseT than it is to replace a MAU. However, there may be a specific reason why Token Ring is required (e.g. it is built in to certain industrial equipment and therefore must be supported), in which case the MAU must be replaced.

MAU

As a MAU is at the centre of Token Ring network it provides the means by which the machines can communicate. Inside the MAU the ports are connected in a ring fashion, and Token Ring frame circulates through the ports. If a machine is active on the port, the frame is passed down to that machine. If there isn't an active machine, the frame bypasses that port. In the event there are more machines than ports on the MAU, multiple MAUs can be connected using the RING IN and RING OUT ports on each. The only real function of a MAU is to make a complete ring from all the active ports. Figure 6.14 shows a MAU implementation. Whilst the wiring appears as a star, the operation is in fact a ring.

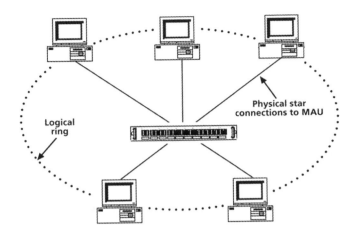

Figure 6.14   Implementation of a MAU

CRUCIAL CONCEPT

It is the method of accessing the ring in Token Ring network rather than the MAU which ensures that bandwidth isn't wasted (see Chapter 5).

Quick test

Briefly identify the function of Token Ring MAU.

Section 8

Interconnection based on a router

Introduction

Routers are perhaps the most important networking device for medium to large-sized networks. Along with switches, they are the main piece of equipment installed. As access to the Internet is based on routers, it is essential to understand their operation and use. Routers are also the most important traffic-regulating devices on large networks.

Routers

Routing devices operate at layer three of the OSI seven-layer model. Working at this layer, the router can make decisions based on network addresses (or logical addresses – see Chapter 3) as opposed to layer two (the MAC address layer). Like a bridge, routers can connect different layer-two technologies, such as FDDI, Ethernet and Token Ring.

The main purpose of a router is to examine the network address (commonly the IP address) of incoming packets, to determine the best path for them through the network (path determination) and to forward them along that path (switching). Because of this capability, routers have become the backbone of the Internet (see Chapter 11).

Routers differ from bridges in several respects. A bridge makes forwarding decisions based upon the MAC address and is therefore only useful *within* a network, whereas routers are used for internetwork communication. As an organisation's network becomes larger, it must to be divided up if it is to retain its performance. As we saw earlier, division by a bridge or switch splits the collision domain. What neither device does, however, is restrict the broadcasts. Broadcasts are a very common and a very necessary feature of a network but need to be contained if bandwidth is not to be compromised – excessive broadcasts lead to what is known as a 'broadcast storm', which consumes large amounts of bandwidth. Because there is no structure to MAC addresses, broadcast containment cannot be achieved by devices operating at layer two (the MAC address layer). Routers operate at the network layer and use the organisation's logical addressing mechanism for forwarding packets only. Hence they contain broadcasts.

Take for example, a typical IP address at the University of Sunderland. The address 157.228.1XX.XXX represents computers inside the School of Computing and Technology and 157.228.2XX.XXX represents the Business School. The 157.228 part of the address identifies the university and the XXX.XXX.1 the School of Computing and Technology and the XXX.XXX.2 the Business School. In this way a meaningful structure can be given to the network. Broadcast frames not intended for the Business School (or vice versa) will be prevented by the router from being sent to that address because they do not contain the XXX.XXX.2. Hence packets can be routed efficiently. This is the basis upon which the Internet works – 157.228. is the address for the University of Sunderland whereas 198.133.219. is the address for Cisco Systems Inc. (IP addresses are controlled by the Network Info Center (NIC) in the USA.)

Routers typically are used to join LANs to the backbone of an organisation's network, thus ensuring that the backbone does not become congested with unnecessary traffic. Figure 6.15 shows such an implementation. Notice how the routers create broadcast domains and how the switches provide collision domains.

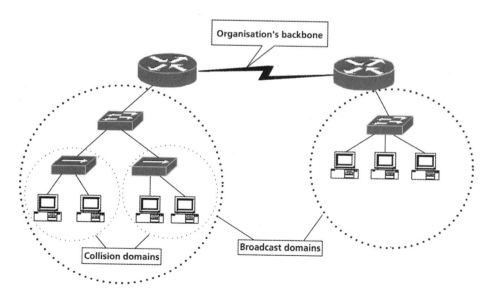

Figure 6.15   Typical implementation of a router

CRUCIAL CONCEPT

Routers enable separate LANs within an organisation to be connected. They provide connectivity whilst keeping the LANs separate, and they contain both broadcasts and collisions.

Quick test

Briefly describe the operation of a router and give examples of where they are commonly deployed.

Section 9

Interconnection based on a gateway

Introduction

Gateways connect two networks together – for example, dissimilar networks such as IBM's Systems Network Architecture (SNA) and DECnet.

Gateway

A gateway can be used to connect together two networks at any layer at or above the network layer. As there was often a large amount of incompatibility between networks supplied by different vendors, more translation was required than that afforded by standard networking devices. Hence gateways were used to overcome this problem. Because of the amount of translation required, Gateways were often slow and more expensive than other interconnecting devices, and they were typically implemented as a software solution on a computer. With developments such as the OSI seven-layer model and schemes such as the Government Open Systems Integration Project (GOSIP), computer manufacturers have opened up their systems to allow interconnection through standard networking devices, thus negating the need for gateways.

Gateways are, however, re-emerging in small office, home office (SOHO) networking where they are often used to connect the home/small office network to the Internet (see Figure 6.16). In this figure machine A is running software to act as a gateway. It has two network connections and is moving traffic between the two networks – the ADSL/cable connection and the SOHO LAN. Such gateways can be established easily using the Internet Connection Sharing option in Microsoft Windows (98SE onwards). In this mode these gateways usually perform the Network Address Translation (NAT) function – they give multiple SOHO machines access to the Internet through the sharing of one IP address from the Internet Service Provider (ISP).

Figure 6.16   SOHO gateway

Quick test

Briefly discuss the purpose of a gateway.

Section 10

End of chapter assessment

This chapter has discussed the major networking devices. Any assessment is likely to ask you either to compare and contrast networking devices or to discuss the operation/typical application of each device.

Question

Name the eight major networking devices and, for each, identify its function and typical application. If appropriate, discuss its abilities to control broadcasts and collisions.

Answer

The assessor is looking for a simple list of the major networking equipment, which is likely to be worth about one mark per item. The main marks are going to come from your discussion of each of the devices. However, seven marks are going simply for writing the list, so you may as well have them. Once you have completed your list, you can start discussing each of the major pieces of kit. For most of the equipment you will find that a diagram will aid your discussion and also make your answer clearer. Ensure that, when you discuss each piece of kit, you identify the layer of the OSI seven-layer model in which it operates; whether it operates on bits, frames or packets, the technology in which it operates; and, if you want extra marks, what effect it has upon collisions and broadcasts. You then simply need to discuss each piece of kit and identify typical applications. Remember to plan out your answer. If you have an hour you can only really spend six minutes discussing each piece of kit if you are to cover them all within the time. However, it is more likely you will be asked to discuss three from a list within half an hour.

Section 11

Further reading and research

See the *www.PhilipIrving.com* website for up-to-date further reading and support for this chapter.

Hodson, P. (2002) *Local Area Networks* (4th edn), Continuum. ISBN: 0 82645 866 1. Chapter 11.
Cisco Networking Academy Program (2001) *First Year Companion Guide* (2nd edn), Cisco Press. ISBN: 1 58713 025 4. Chapters 3 and 30.

Microsoft Windows Help – look under Internet Connection Sharing or ICS.

Chapter 7
Network design process

Chapter summary

The costs of installing a network are high – not only in terms of equipment and materials but also in terms of installing the media and the disruption to the organisation. Most organisations are also critically dependent upon their networks, which means they can neither afford for it not to work nor to have further disruptions to repair problems. Network design is the process of analysing an organisation, its current network, its needs and its plans for the future. From this, a networking solution can be produced that will meet the organisation's current and immediate future needs and that can be introduced incrementally. Network design is a specialist process and so this chapter can only provide an overview of what is involved. This should be sufficient for assessment purposes.

Learning outcomes

After stuyding this chapter you should aim to test your achievement of the following outcomes. You should be able to:

Outcome 1: Network design goals
Understand the four main requirements of network design. Question 1 at the end of this chapter will test you on this.

Outcome 2: Design components
Understand how the positioning of devices and servers can boost network performance. Question 2 at the end of this chapter will test you on this.

Outcome 3: Methodology
Understand and be able to apply a methodology for the analysis of a network. Question 3 at the end of this chapter will test you on this.

Outcome 4: Capacity planning
Understand and be able to apply a methodology for capacity planning within a network. Question 4 at the end of this chapter will test you on this.

Outcome 5: Sample design
Apply the methodologies to a typical scenario. Question 5 at the end of this chapter will test you on this.

How will you be assessed on this?

Design is normally assessed as an assignment as it does not lend itself to being assessed through an exam. In an assignment, you will often be placed in a group where you will be given a scenario and asked to produce a solution to the problem the scenario poses. This will almost always contain some kind of capacity planning (an example is given in Chapter 12). Design questions in an exam or TCT tend to be limited to a discussion of the process; they rarely include capacity planning. However, if capacity planning is on the syllabus, it may well be tested.

Section 1

Network design goals

In any design process, it is essential to understand the goals of the design before you begin.

Network design goals

Network design is a complex and challenging task. There are many things that must be established and analysed if a network design is to be successful. A network should not be judged simply in terms of its size: a network that contains only a small number of nodes can have stringent design requirements. The goals of network design will vary according to the client organisation and the design contractors. However, the following four criteria are a good starting point.

Functionality
The network must do what it is supposed to do. It must do this reliably and at an appropriate speed. Issues here include performance, reliability and correct functionality. Ultimately, the users of the network must be able to carry out their tasks efficiently and effectively.

Scalability
One thing that is known for certain about today's networks is that they must change to fit tomorrow's requirements. On average, an organisation undergoes a major reorganisation every three years, and the network must be able to adapt to such changes. The network must be able to grow incrementally – i.e. grow without the need for any major changes to the overall design.

Adaptability
Adaptability has two aspects – the network's ability to adapt to changes in the organisation and the network's ability to embrace technological change. Networking is the fastest-growing area of computing and, as such, is continually developing. Any proposed networking solution should do nothing to limit the implementation of new technologies as and when they become available.

Manageability
Networks need to be managed after their implementation. A well designed network should facilitate ease of monitoring and management.

Quick test

Briefly discuss the four basic requirements of good network design.

Section 2

Network design components

Designing a network is not just about the cabling and the network devices but about the positioning of servers and access to the data they hold. As we saw in Chapter 6, the different network devices provide a range of services, from network interconnection to collision and broadcast containment. Hence a good design will ensure the network does not suffer from excess collisions, can contain broadcasts and that all nodes will be able to communicate at the planned level of performance.

Network design components

As we have already noted, network performance and network technologies are constantly changing, and so designers need to ensure the LANs they design can accommodate these changes and that performance is maximised by the careful positioning of critical components. When designing for high-speed technologies and multimedia-based applications, network designers need to address the following critical components of LAN design:

- The function and positioning of servers.
- Collision detection/segmentation.

Function and positioning of servers

Servers fall into two distinct classes:

- Organisational servers (such as email servers or DNS).
- Workgroup servers (data and applications).

A good designer takes great care over the positioning of servers and of who will access them. Figure 7.1 shows a well designed network where the workgroup servers (A & B) have been placed close to where they will be used and where the email server has been placed at organisational level. By structuring the network in this way, the machines connected to switch A can use server A without having to use the network backbone (through the organisational-level switch), thus keeping traffic on the backbone to a minimum. If they need access to email, these machines will not cause excess traffic on the machines connected to switch B whilst accessing the organisational server (for email). Access to server B from the machines connected to switch A is possible but should not be used often. This type of design is known as a two-layer network design and is suitable for small enterprises.

Figure 7.1   The positioning of servers

Notice there is no router in Figure 7.1. This could create broadcast-related problems. Because there are no routers, a broadcast by any machine will traverse the whole network, hence wasting bandwidth. The solution would be to replace the organisational-level switch with a router, which would divide the network into two broadcast domains (Figure 7.2).

Figure 7.2   Router now divides the two networks into two separate broadcast domains

Collision detection/segmentation

As we saw in Chapter 6, collisions can be a real problem with Ethernet networks. Indeed, during heavy loads collisions can reduce the available bandwidth to 35%. This is because the nodes contend with one another for access to the network. The designer of an ethernet network aims to position the equipment in such a way as to reduce access contention and the number of collisions on the network. The single most important device for this purpose is the switch. In Figure 7.1 the switch virtually eliminates collisions on each network (A and B) and also on the organisational backbone. Hence Figure 7.1 shows the correct positioning of switches if they are to reduce collisions. This process is known as **segmentation**. In a coaxial ethernet network, bridges provide collision control.

CRUCIAL TIP

Introducing switches into the network segments the network into separate collision domains but does not contain broadcasts.

CRUCIAL CONCEPT

The correct positioning of servers is crucial to network design. If the servers are badly placed traffic may have to traverse the entire network, hence reducing overall performance.

Quick test

Explain why the positioning of servers is of critical importance in network design. Also discuss why designers should consider collision detection and segmentation when designing networks.

Section 3

Network design methodology

Network design is similar, in many ways, to systems analysis and design. The designer needs to:

- gather facts and figures about the organisation and user requirements and expectations;
- analyse the requirements of the network;
- design the structure;
- document the network.

Gathering facts and figures

This process involves finding out as much about the organisation as possible: its size, current status, plans for the building, plans for the future, number of current employees, plans for growth/downsizing, software in use, future software requirements (e.g. changing to a new computer system), management procedures, office procedures, the views of the people who will be using the network, etc.

CRUCIAL TIP

While there are a great many things to find out about an organisation that is considering a new network design, an assessor will want to see that you appreciate the importance of facts and figures – size of data files, number of users or plans to move to a new building, etc.

It should also be established whether data or software are mission critical. It would likewise be necessary to determine what desktop computers are allowed on the network and if there are any protocols that need to be supported. If addresses or names are to be allocated to the machines, it has to be established who in the organisation controls such lists.

Analysing requirements

The information collected must then be analysed. Particular attention should be paid to the requirements of the network over its lifetime – for example, does the organisation plan to expand rapidly in the near future? User requirements should also be analysed carefully to ensure the network will be able to deliver what the users want within the time frame they want it. If this is not possible, the end users' expectations need to be managed to ensure the delivered network is not a disappointment. Perhaps the most important question to ask here is: how can you tell if a network is successful?

In analysing requirements, the network's availability should be determined. Availability is a measure of the following:

- **Throughput** – how much throughput the organisation expects from the network.
- **Response time** – the time the users expect to wait before the network provides them with the information they require.
- **Access to resources** – what resources the users expect to have access to, and what the organisational policy is on access to resources. This often has to be balanced to provide an effective network.
- **Reliability** – a realistic expectation of the network's reliability (100% reliability can be expensive to achieve!).

Organisations that demand high availability will need to carry the costs of such availability – redundant links, spare equipment, etc. However, the network's required capacity must be planned for (see Section 5 below).

Designing the structure of the network

The network structure relates to:

- the network's topology;
- the network's cabling;
- the connection of devices.

The first two points are, surprisingly, quite straightforward. Current EIA/TIA recommendations state that networks implemented using a star topology should have a minimum of two networking points to every desktop (not all need to be live). EIA/TIA also require that a Wiring Closet (WC) should be placed on each floor to serve no more than 1000 m². Where floor size exceeds this, two or more wiring closets should be used. EIA/TIA also specify that a wiring closet should have the following:

- Sufficient heating/cooling to maintain a temperature of 21°C when the equipment is in full operation.
- A minimum of two non-switched dedicated AC outlets (positioned every 1.8 m along the wall at a height of 150 mm above the floor).
- The floor can take the weight of networking equipment.
- Light fixtures should provide 200 lux of brightness and be at least 2.6 m above the ground. The switch should be immediately inside the door. If the light used is fluorescent, it should be clear of the cable runs (because of interference).
- A door 0.9 m wide that opens outwards with a lock to allow anyone inside the room to exit at any time (this may need to be adjusted in the light of local fire regulations).

To determine the best location for the wiring closet, a map of the building should be annotated showing the proposed layout of the computers. Using the above checklist, the potential locations of the wiring closets are marked on the plan. Using a compass, a 50 m circle with the potential closet at its centre is drawn to see if all the computers will fit inside this circle. If not, another location must be chosen or, alternatively, more than one closet may be needed. Even though the maximum cable length in 100BaseT is 100 m, a 50 m radius allows for awkward runs, corner turns, etc. A patch panel lead and a lead to a desktop, will all increase the overall length.

For the main wiring closet (the one that will provide any external connections), it is recommended that the telecomms provider's is used where their cable enters the building (this entry point is known as the Point of Presence (POP)). This wiring closet is known as the Main Distribution Facility (MDF); the others are known as Intermediate Distribution Facilities (IDFs). EIA/TIA also recommend that the cabling is category 5 to the desktop and either fibre or copper between the wiring closets.

'Standard' design structures

As the popularity of networks increases, a standard design structure is emerging based on two or three-layer models. As discussed earlier, a two-layer model is suitable for small organisations. Such networks are effectively divided into two layers (see Figure 7.3). The bottom layer (the access layer) provides access to the network's services. In the access layer are the computers that are to use the network and their servers. These are arranged in groups so that the machines that need the services from workgroup server A are on the same switch as the server. The bulk of the traffic in these groups should never need to leave the workgroup environment. Only email and cross-workgroup traffic needs to pass into the distribution layer. This keeps the distribution layer free from unnecessary traffic, thus helping performance. The distribution layer distributes services to the organisation – in this case, cross-workgroup connectivity and access to email. The distribution layer may well form the backbone of a university/college campus or the backbone of an entire building.

Figure 7.3   Standard two-level network design

Often an organisation has multiple sites spread over a wide geographical area. In such cases, a further layer is added above the distribution layer. Known as the core layer, this layer provides fast, wide-area connections between geographically remote sites. For example, the University of Sunderland has two main campuses – the St Peter's Campus and the City Campus. The two are about 2 miles apart. Using a three-layer model, there are distribution layers at both campuses (effectively acting as the campus backbone) and a core layer connecting the two campuses (see Figure 7.4).

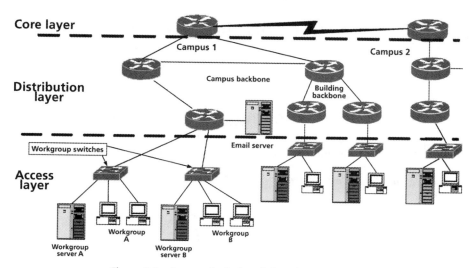

Figure 7.4   A correctly designed three-layer network

--- CRUCIAL TIP ---

These standard layouts should be followed when designing a network.

Documenting the network

The design and implementation stages of the network should be well documented. This documentation will be the starting point should there be a need for troubleshooting. Hence the documentation should provide:

- detailed maps of the wiring closets;
- details of the machines attached to these wiring closets;
- details of the type and quantity of cables used to connect to the IDFs;
- notes about any spare cables and their location;
- details about cabling between IDFs/MDFs.

Troubleshooting is a very stressful task. Therefore, the better the documentation, the faster the network is likely to be brought back up. Documentation should as be full as possible. Also, bearing in mind that 80% of networking problems are caused by layer one (cables, connectors, etc.), the leads need to be documented very carefully.

CRUCIAL CONCEPT

To be effective, a network must be well designed. An essential step in this process is to gather and analyse information. An organisation's network is likely to be mission critical and so any faults must be repaired immediately. Correcting faults and upgrading the network are far easier if there is sufficient, up-to-date documentation.

Quick test

Briefly outline network design methodology.

Section 4

Capacity planning

Capacity planning ensures there will be sufficient capacity in the new network for it to be able to cope with the demands placed upon it. Measuring the capacity of the current network can help to identify performance issues and can also guide the design process.

CRUCIAL TIP

Most questions designed to test your knowledge of capacity planning will start with a set of numbers, that, when used in a capacity plan, produce a problem. The assessors are testing your ability to spot this problem. They write an assignment and deliberately hide figures in the text – a good designer is always on the lookout for hidden information! You should read the assignment thoroughly and highlight every number mentioned.

The capacity planning process

Capacity planning has two purposes: to measure the load on the current network and to estimate the load that might be imposed on the proposed network. Sophisticated tools are available to help with this process but it is more likely you will be required to measure these loads mathematically. The maths involved in capacity planning is relatively straightfoward. It is used to determine:

- the current load on the network;
- the proposed/additional load on the network;

- if there is enough capacity in the network to cope;
- if there are likely to be any peak-time problems (i.e. when the traffic is at its highest, will the network be able to cope?).

To do this, as much numerical information as possible is collected:

- How many computers are connected/to be connected?
- What packages do they use?
- Are the packages held centrally or locally?
- How often are they downloaded?
- What is their size?
- What sort of data is downloaded?
- How often?
- What is its size?
- How often do the users print out from the network?
- What kind of printer do they use? (Postscript printers put a huge load on a network and should be avoided.)
- What are the file sizes?
- Does a file go directly to a printer or to a computer and then to a printer (in which case it is on the network twice)?
- What about email/Internet traffic?
- How often are they used?
- What are they used for?

This should provide enough information about the amount of traffic moved by the network.

However, unless sophisticated software is used to carry out these measurements, the figures obtained will be an educated guess. Allowances should be made for the frame/packet headers, which will be added to the data as it passes down the layers of the seven-layer model (see Chapter 4). It will be necessary to talk to suppliers about any proposed applications and, possibly, obtain copies of the software to evaluate the load before purchase. The equipment connected to the network and its operation should be checked in case it imposes a load on the network.

CRUCIAL TIP

File sizes are measured in bytes and network traffic is measured in bits. Remember to multiply bytes by 8 to get bits. Thus a 1 MB file is 8 Mb.

As much information as possible about the organisation itself must also be collected:

- How long does the organisation use its network each day (if it is open 9–5 then it's 8 hours)?
- What does it use its network for?
- Do the users work flexi-time or do they all have the same start and finish time?
- Are there any problems with the current network?
- If so, what weeks/days/times do these problems occur?
- Is there any other pattern to them?
- What time is lunch?
- Does everyone leave together for lunch?
- What is the pattern of the working day (is it like a school/college/university where activities change on an hourly basis)?
- Are backups of the network servers taken at night? Is this across the network?

This should provide enough information about the time period over which the traffic needs to be shipped.

Finally, the design parameters must be established:

- What is the anticipated lifespan of the network?
- Will there be any anticipated growth/decline in the organisation's activities during the network's lifespan?
- Does the building itself contain any physical constraints (e.g. solid floor or ceilings, lots of electric motors, etc. that will cause interference)?
- Should the network be a LAN only or a WAN/LAN?
- Is any existing network equipment to be retained?
- What finance is available?
- What integration is required with other systems/networks/hardware?

Quality of service (QoS) also needs to be determined. QoS basically means the design parameters we noted in Section 3 – the responses users expect, the network's reliability, security issues, etc.

This process should provide enough information to begin the capacity planning. Remember, answers are needed to two questions:

- Can the network cope at present?
- Will it be able to cope with the proposed changes?

For each question, it must be determined whether the network can cope with:

the daily load (normally the answer to this is 'yes');
peak-time load problems (usually more tricky to answer).

Peak times are when the network is under the most strain – for example, when a class begins at college at least one class will log into the network and download software and data to begin their work. Obviously the students and instructors wish to begin as soon as possible but, the network is probably under its heaviest load during that period – a peak-time problem. (Section 5 gives an example capacity plan for a college and discusses the issues raised in this.)

─────────── CRUCIAL CONCEPT ───────────

Capacity plans are only as good as the information gathered. Time should be spent collecting and analysing carefully all the relevant data.

Quick test

Briefly outline the stages involved in capacity planning.

Section 5

Sample design

Introduction

In this section we will consider Irving's College of Technology (ICT) to analyse the current problems they are having with their network. We will discuss these problems and propose some solutions. ICT have an IT suite but are having problems with the performance of the network in this suite. What follows is an excerpt from a real assignment I used a couple of years ago.

The 50 computers in the IT suite are networked with two Novell servers using two segments of 10Base2 ethernet separated by a repeater. The QoS the college required was for the machines to be operational within five minutes of the class starting. Primarily, the machines run a package known as Trainoffice. Trainoffice offers a simulated office environment. In terms of network load, each machine loads the software (30 MB); uses 20 MB of data and, on average, each user prints 10 MB per session. Data is loaded from two Novell servers (old 486 machines). Unfortunately, such are the problems with this suite that it has been closed temporarily. The principal is very disappointed about this as the machines in the suite are the most modern of all the college's computers. It can be assumed that classes in the IT suite change every hour.

Process

Although the above is only a paragraph, it contains lots of information. The first thing to note is that the IT suite has been temporarily closed because of the problems (not a good sign!) and that the classes change every hour. Thus the capacity planning involves *60 minute intervals* – everything needs to be loaded, printed, saved, etc., in that time frame.

Next we need to consider the figures:

- 50 computers.
- 30 MB of software.
- 20 MB of data.
- 10 MB printed (through a Novell server; therefore 10 MB to the server followed by 10 MB to the printer – twice the load!).
- 10 Mbps is the theoretical maximum from 10Base2 (7 Mbps actual).
- QoS of five minutes.
- 486 architecture in the servers, which means they can only ship 8 Mbps to the networking card (no PCI architecture).
- Software and data have to be loaded before startup.

So 50 computers × (30 MB software + 20 MB data) = 2500 MB which, times 8, = 20 000 Mb of data to be loaded before startup. We will add 10% to this to allow for packet overheads (headers, CRCs, etc.). Thus the total is now *22 000 Mb*. Before getting into difficulty, 10Base2 can handle 7 Mbps; after that point it may drop to 3.5 Mbps. 22 000 Mb/7 Mbps = 3142 seconds. Thus, assuming the network can handle steadily 7 Mbps it will take 3142 seconds or (53 minutes) for all the machines in the IT suite to be ready to start a 60-minute class! Then they will need to save their data and, possibly, print.

There are two possibilities to overcome these problems:

- Break up the current network with bridges and additional servers to make smaller networks that will perform better.
- Install a brand-new network based on a faster technology that will also have better future proofing.

Excluding the cabling costs, the second option is likely to be cheaper than the first and also more satisfactory. My preference would be for the second option.

We need to examine the load under 100BaseT: 22 000 Mb/100 Mbps = 220 seconds/60 = 3.66 minutes. Thus, with a 100BaseT network, the suite would be operational within about 4 minutes (subject to the server being able to handle the load). Deploying this network would require a different topology, new servers (the old cannot make use of 100 Mbps cards), new cards in the PCs and switching equipment. Switches usually come in 24 or 48 port and so we would require at least two switches. If we installed the two-tier architecture we looked at in Section 2, we would need three 24-port switches and a further switch to join the three switches. The scenario mentions servers, and the best solution would be to incorporate three workgroup servers (as shown in Figure 7.5), each attached to a switch, along with 17 machines (even though this would mean, in effect, only 16 machines!). The new loading would be: 17 machines $\times$ 50 MB = 850 MB + 10% = 935 MB $\times$ 8 = 7480 Mb / 100 Mbps = 75 seconds for the machines to become operational. This includes no margin for error but, assuming 100% was left for contingency, this is still only 150 seconds, half the QoS of 5 minutes.

Figure 7.5   Proposed design for ICT

Printing and saving must also be accommodated – this will usually be distributed in the lesson but may also come near the end; if it does, then it is a peak time problem. Assume that 20 MB needs to be saved: 17 machines $\times$ 20 MB = 340 MB + 10% = 374 MB $\times$ 8 = 2992 Mb/100 = 30 seconds. The printing needs to traverse the network to the server and then from the server to the printer (it may be on the network twice so allowances must be made for this or it needs to be investigated more fully). This is ambiguous, so assume the worst-case scenario that it is on the network twice: 17 $\times$ (2 $\times$ 20 MB) = 680 MB + 10% = 748 MB $\times$ 8 = 5984 Mb/100 = 59.84 seconds. Thus the proposed network will handle the load imposed adequately. Had this been an organisation that did not change its activities every the hour, this could have been taken across the working day (8 hours?), but peak times should still be noted – arriving in the morning, lunchtime and printing late in the day.

Average load

In this scenario, everything needs to be completed within a one-hour period. To calculate the average load (which is rarely a problem) we divide the total data by the time period. In the 100BaseT final design we have: 17 machines $\times$ (30 MB applications + 20 MB load + 20 MB save + (2 $\times$ 10 MB print)) = 1530 MB; 1530 MB $\times$ 8 = 12 240 Mb. There are 60 minutes $\times$ 60 seconds in an hour = 3600. 12 240 Mb period load/3600 seconds in a period = 3.4 Mbps average load. This is well within the capacity of our network.

CRUCIAL CONCEPT

Remember, the time taken to get all the computers operational can be calculated approximately by the following formula:

$$\frac{\text{Total data and/or software to be downloaded before work can begin (in megabits)}}{\text{Maximum throughput of the technology}}$$

Remember to use megabits and to add 10% to the load to allow for packet headers, etc.

The average load on the network per day/session can be calculated approximately by the following formula:

$$\frac{\text{Total data/software/printing of entire day/session}}{\text{No. of seconds in day/session}}$$

Quick test

Carefully work though the figures without looking at the calculations given here. Do you get the same answer? If not, where did you go wrong?

Section 6

End of chapter assessment

Questions

1. Outline the major things that must be taken into consideration when undertaking a network design.
2. Discuss how the positioning of networking devices and equipment is fundamental to good network design.
3. There are four basic steps in network design methodology. Name these four steps and discuss each.
4. Discuss the process of capacity planning and outline how you would undertake this process for an organisation.
5. Prove that the figures shown below provide a startup time of almost 21 minutes and an average hourly load of 2.5 Mbps:

   - 25 computers;
   - 30 MB software;
   - 10 MB data (both software and data must be downloaded before the machines can be used);
   - 1 hour time slot;
   - 10Base2 networking.

Rerun the above example to show that the same load can be handled by 100BaseT in less than two minutes.

Answers

1. To answer this question you need to name and discuss briefly the four main goals of network design: functionality, scalability, adaptability and manageability. You need to demonstrate that you understand the importance of each of the terms to the process of network design. Remember these represent the goals of network design.

2. This question requires you to demonstrate your knowledge about the positioning of networking devices. You should discuss why the positioning of networking devices is critical to the best performance of the network. You should also discuss what the two types of server are, and what is meant by the terms 'collision' and 'broadcast domains'. Ideally, you should illustrate your answer with diagrams that show the correct placement of both workgroup and organisational servers. You should also give examples of how the correct positioning of the various types of networking devices will create collision and broadcast domains and explain the expected benefits of this.

3. This question is in two parts. The first asks you to name the four basic steps in network design methodology. This serves as a guide to help you structure the rest of the question, but you will gain marks for simply naming them. The second part asks you to discuss each of the steps. There is plenty to discuss and so you should plan your answer carefully so you don't run out of time. You should ensure you explain that this as a sequential procedure and you should stress the importance of gathering all the facts and of correct analysis and design. Most network designers scrimp on the documentation, which is bad practice – especially when 80% of all network problems occur at layer one. You should stress the importance of good documentation and its value when something goes wrong.

4. The important thing to note about this question is that it is asking you not only to discuss the process of capacity planning but also to embellish your answer by discussing how you would undertake capacity planning for an organisation. You need to discuss the four steps in the process of capacity planning, detailing the figures you need to calculate the current and required load. You should identify the timespan under consideration – the example in the chapter had a one-hour interval. You also need to discuss how you would determine if there is enough capacity in the network to cope with both peak loads and the daily/session requirements. The assessor would not expect you to undertake the maths but would expect an explanation of how you would determine the current and required capacity, both for peak times and for the daily load.

5. This question is very specific. The assessor is asking you to calculate two types of capacity plan: one showing the length of time it will take for the machines to become operational (software and data to be loaded), the other showing the average load across the time period (1 hour). The formulae are given in the crucial concept box at the end of Section 5. The question also contains the answer and you are asked to prove it.

Time to start:

$$\frac{((25 \times ((10 \text{ MB} + 30 \text{ MB}) \times 8)) + 10\%)}{7 \text{ Mbps*}} = 21 \text{ minutes}$$

(*This should be replaced by 100 Mbps when re-running the calculation for 100BaseT.)

Average load:

$$\frac{((25 \times ((10 \text{ MB} + 30 \text{ MB}) \times 8)) + 10\%)}{3600 \text{ seconds}} = 2.5 \text{ Mbps}$$

The average load will be the same on 100BaseT as the network speed is not taken into account in this calculation.

Section 7

Further reading and research

See the *www.PhilipIrving.com* website for up-to-date further reading and support for this chapter.

Cisco Networking Academy Program (2001) *First Year Companion Guide* (2nd edn). Cisco Press. ISBN: 1 58713 025 4. Chapter 4.

Cisco Networking Academy Program (2001) *Second Year Companion Guide* (2nd edn). Cisco Press. ISBN: 1 58713 029 7. Chapter 8.

Hodson, P. (2002) *Local Area Networks* (4th edn). Continuum. ISBN: 0 82645 866 1. Chapters 13 and 14.

Chapter 8
Network software

Chapter summary

This chapter is the first of three that look at the role, setup and management of a typical network server. The hardware and software that comprise a network facilitate the exchange of data and applications. Perhaps the most important piece of hardware is the server. Most organisations deploy either a Windows-based server or a UNIX-based server. Here we will concentrate on UNIX, for two main reasons:

- UNIX provides greater scalability and is therefore used in large organisations.
- A public domain version of UNIX (Linux) is available which will enable you to practise installing a networked operating system at a low cost.

Learning outcomes

After studying this chapter you should aim to test your achievement of the following outcomes. You should be able to:

Outcome 1: Multi-user operating systems
Understand the main features of multi-user, multi-tasking operating systems. Question 1 at the end of this chapter will test you on this.

Outcome 2: The UNIX filing structure
Understand the filing structure used in a UNIX filing system. Question 2 at the end of this chapter will test you on this.

Outcome 3: Filing system security
Understand and be able to manage security in a file server environment. Question 3 at the end of this chapter will test you on this.

How will you be assessed on this?

This subject area lends itself quite well to exam-type assessments rather than assignments. As there are many questions that could be asked about this subject, you should make sure you understanding what is covered in this chapter well in advance of any examinations. You may also be assessed in your practical ability to set up a NOS.

Section 1

Multi-user operating systems

Computers that act as servers must be able to cope with the access demands of many different users and also be able to provide these users with the services they require. Servers vary in their capability to do this depending on the operating system that has been installed. UNIX enables users to access files and it also processes on their behalf. Multi-user operating systems also vary in the way in which jobs are given access to the processor. It is important you understand the basics of multi-user operating systems as these are important not only in the world of work but also in the world of exams!

Peer-to-peer networks

As we have noted throughout this book, the whole point of networks is to facilitate the exchange of data and software. As we saw in Chapter 1, this exchange can be accomplished through peer-to-peer networking, such as Windows 98, 2000 and XP. However, as noted earlier, peer-to-peer networks are only suitable for small networking situations. Once an organisation reaches the limit of its peer-to-peer network, it must consider installing a server.

Multi-user operating systems

Larger organisations or those that have outgrown a peer-to-peer network must make use of a server. As all the users will depend upon the performance of the machine chosen to be the server, the server's operating system must be suitable for multi-user tasking: it must be able to undertake more than one job at a time for more than one user at a time. UNIX is a good example of such an operating system as it enables a hundred users each to have ten jobs active at the same time.

Needless to say, multi-user, multi-tasking operating systems are extremely complex. They are responsible for such tasks as:

- job scheduling;
- the allocation of resources;
- hardware operations;
- user operations;
- protecting the user's work;
- protecting each user's working memory;
- providing disk storage and quotas for each user;
- running each user's various jobs.

Multi-user, multi-tasking operating systems can be classified into two groups, depending on the way jobs are given access to the processor.

Non-pre-emptive systems
Non-pre-emptive operating systems wait until a job quits the processor voluntarily. Should this job go into a loop and therefore not quit the processor, no other job will be allowed access to the processor. The server is thus hung and would need to be rebooted. Early versions of Novell Netware operated on this principle.

Pre-emptive systems
Pre-emptive operating systems are more complex. A job is given a time slice for acces to the processor. If the job does not quit the processor voluntarily, it will be removed once its time slice is up. Even though it is given another time slice its access is suspended whilst other jobs have their turn on the processor. As this type of operating system is robust a looping job will not take the processor down. It is also a fairer method of access as each job is given a turn without having to wait for the previous job(s) to finish. UNIX is an example of such a system.

CRUCIAL CONCEPT

Servers that offers pre-emptive scheduling afford greater resilience to rogue software.

Quick test

Briefly discuss the features you would expect from a multi-user, multi-tasking operating system.

Section 2

The UNIX filing structure

Multi-user operating systems have large and complex filing systems, and UNIX is no exception. UNIX can support a great many hard disks, and even many computers, inside its filing system. This means an entire organisation can be housed within one filing system. It is important to note, however, that a filing system on a large machine is not restricted to the size of its hard disk drive.

Directory structures

In DOS or Windows, the filing system is based on the physical disk drive – if there are two 40 GB disk drives these are assigned a drive identifier (e.g. drive C) and access to the information on these drives is obtained by using these letters. This system works quite well with filing systems that fit on to a physical drive but, in large multi-user systems, such a huge amount of data needs to be stored it will not fit on one physical drive. Hence the filing system in UNIX is not drive based. Instead, there is one filing structure to embrace the entire filing system. This system might be the entire organisation, one department or even specific areas within one department. UNIX's filing system can span multiple physical disk drives or even multiple machines (see Figure 8.1).

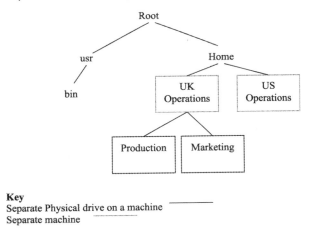

Key
Separate Physical drive on a machine ——————
Separate machine ······················

Figure 8.1   UNIX directory structure

This filing system is spread across three machines. The machine being accessed hosts the /usr/bin directory, whilst the home directory is split across two physical machines, one housing UK operations and the other US operations. It is possible for these machines to be located in their respective countries but still to provide access from one to the other. This is possible through the Networked Filing System (NFS) – a UNIX protocol that allows filing systems to be distributed, but yet accessible, throughout an entire network.

Many UNIX machines use the principle of logical volumes. Essentially, a logical volume is a way of joining two or more physical disks. For example, if a company has a corporate database of 120 GB but the only drives available are 80 GB. If this database must be contained on one disk only there will be a problem. The solution is to create one logical volume spanning two physical drives (Figure 8.2). The database can then be saved to the logical volume rather than the physical disk (or volume).

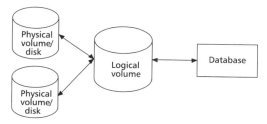

Figure 8.2   Logical volumes

Quick test

Briefly discuss the UNIX filing system, highlighting the differences between this system and a filing system you are familiar with.

Section 3

Filing system security

Users and groups

When multiple users have access to a filing system, individual users' files must be protected. For instance, the managing director of a company would not be pleased if all the staff had access to the personnel records, etc. To provide this protection, UNIX uses the idea of file owners and groups: access permissions can be set for both owners and groups. In this way, the UNIX filing systems can provide file protection and security. Unlike DOS or some versions of Windows, the files stored on a UNIX machine can belong to any user. However, some files will be confidential whilst others will require wider access – perhaps to project groups or even everyone on the system. For example, a company intranet should be accessible to everyone in the organisation but budgetary information might be restricted to senior management. Using the principle of file owners and groups, UNIX supports such access, and Figure 8.3 shows a directory listing where the owner of the file (cs0pir) and the group to which the file belongs (staff) have been highlighted.

```
$ ls -lisa|more
total 6963
    7324902    2 -rw- - - - - - - 1 cs0pir staff    25 Mar 23 11:53 #fred#
    7324800    8 drwx–x–x 46 cs0pir staff    3584 May 30 12:30 .
    7324817    2 lrwxrwxrwx 1 cs0pir staff    36 Mar 23 11:52 .#fred ->
cs0pir@isis.sunderland.ac.uk.16165:1
      2 1 dr-xr-xr-x 21 root root    21 May 30 12:51 ..
    7324877    2 -rw-r–r– 1 cs0pir staff  446 Jun 27 1997 .ab_library
    7324882    2 -rw-r–r– 1 cs0pir staff    141 Jun 27 1997 .ab_library.lock
    7328640    2 drwxr-xr-x 2 cs0pir staff    512 Sep 23 1994 .cetables
    7324804    2 -rw-r–r– 1 cs0pir staff    747 Mar 8 1996 .cshrc
```

Figure 8.3   Users and groups

The systems administrator is usually a superuser (the root account in UNIX). The superuser has unrestricted privileges and access to all files and directories (the superuser account is used in Chapter 9 to set up a UNIX system).

Rights

To the left of the owner and group information in Figure 8.3 is information about the file's rights. For example:

-rwxr–r-x

The first character denotes that it is either a file (-), a directory (d) or a link (l). The following three characters represent the owner's rights in this case rwx indicating that the user has read, write and execute permissions to the file. The second group of three characters represents the rights of the group – in this case members of the group this file belongs to can only read the file. The final three characters represent the rights of the rest of the world – in this case, read and execute.

To change the permissions the systems administrator or the file's owner uses the chmod command. There are essentially two ways of using this command but the easiest and most common way is to use the following criteria to determine the value of the rights to be added and then to use the command below to add them:

Right required	Value
Read	4
Write	2
Execute (search if the target is a directory)	1

chmod abc <filename>

In this command, a indicates the rights of the owner, b the rights of the group and c the rights of the rest of the world. To allocate more than one right, the values are simply added together: for read and execute this is 4 + 1 = 5. Thus the command to give all rights to all users would be chmod 777 <filename>. For web pages, chmod 755 * is normally used. This gives the owner rwx, the group r-x and the rest of the world r-x to all files in that directory (* is the wildcard mask). Rights can be applied equally to both files and directories. Ownership of the file can usually only be changed by the systems administrator through the use of the chown command; the group can be changed by the systems administrator or the owner using the chgrp command (Figure 8.4).

```
mainserve:/home/phil/crucial/test % ls -l
total 2
-rw- - - - - - - 1 phil staff      69 Nov 22 16:57 myfile
mainserve:/home/phil/crucial/test % chgrp student myfile
mainserve:/home/phil/crucial/test % ls -l
total 2
-rw - - - - - - - 1 phil student 69 Nov 22 16:57 myfile
mainserve:/home/phil/crucial/test %
```

Figure 8.4   Changing groups

Inherited rights

For even tighter security, it is possible to set default rights that are given to a file upon its creation. Known as inherited rights, this is achieved using the umask command in UNIX. The major advantage of using such a command is that it removes the need for the user to ensure that the file is appropriately protected. However, care must be taken that such files are not made accessible to the group or the world by accident. This can be quite difficult for an inexperienced user.

The umask command sets the default permissions given to newly created files. The first digit defines the rights value to be subtracted from the owner permissions (which cannot be modified). The following two digits define the rights of the group and the world, respectively. Thus the command umask 077 does not alter the rights of the owner but removes all the rights of the group and the world. The command umask 022 removes write access from the group and the world. Figure 8.5 shows an example of the umask command in operation.

```
$
$ umask
022
$ date > date.txt
$ ls -l date.txt
-rw-r--r-- 1 phil staff          34 Apr 26 11:34 date.txt
$ umask 077
$ date > date2.txt
$ ls -l dat*.*
-rw-r--r-- 1 phil staff          34 Apr 26 11:34 date.txt
-rw- - - - - - - 1 phil staff    34 Apr 26 11:34 date2.txt
$
```

Figure 8.5   The umask command in operation

Setting up security on files and directories

The file owner and group commands form the heart of file system security in the UNIX operating system. The operating system checks the access rights of a user who is trying to access a file and allows only the access specified. It is, however, also possible to combine the directory permissions and the file permissions to increase security. For example, by removing the read attributes from a directory, it is possible to prevent users from seeing the contents of the directory they are accessing. To acccess this directory, the user must specify the entire path and the filename. In Figure 8.6, the contents of the test2 directory can be listed but, in the shaded line, all rights except execute have been removed. The owner can now only list the files if he or she knows the entire path and the filename.

```
mainserve:/home/phil/crucial/test % ls -l
total 2
drwxr-xr-x 2 phil staff          512 Nov 22 17:02 test2
mainserve:/home/phil/crucial/test % ls -l test2
total 2
-rw- - - - - - - 1 phil staff    111 Nov 22 17:04 myfile
mainserve:/home/phil/crucial/test % chmod 100 test2
mainserve:/home/phil/crucial/test % ls -l test2
test2: Permission denied
total 2
mainserve:/home/phil/crucial/test % cat ./test2/myfile
This is a really quck test to show you how files can be protected by altering
the attributes of the directory.
mainserve:/home/phil/crucial/test %
```

Figure 8.6   Protecting a file by disallowing directory listings

Other file and directory attributes

In addition to the file attributes given above, UNIX also has attributes for hidden and compressed files.

In UNIX, files are hidden in rather an odd fashion – the filename is preceded by a full stop (.). Thus such files as .profile, .chsrc, etc., aren't seen when a simple directory-listing command is used (ls -l). To see these files, the -a (all argument) command must be used. Files that are compressed in UNIX are given the extension .z. Thus myfile.z is a compressed version of myfile.

Quick test

Briefly outline how files are protected in the UNIX operating system.

Section 4

End of chapter assessment

Questions

1. Discuss the main features of a multi-user operating system.
2. Discuss how the filing structure of a typical multi-user machine, UNIX, is organised.
3. Discuss how filing system security is achieved in the UNIX operating system. Wherever possible, illustrate your answers with examples or commands.

Answers

1. To answer this question, you need to demonstrate your knowledge of multi-user operating system features. Although the question doesn't call for a direct comparison, it is worth mentioning that a multi-user operating system is much more complex than smaller, peer-to-peer ones. You should also mention the functions a multi-user operating system needs to provide and should discuss the two types of scheduling. You should mention the fact that these two types of scheduling are very important as they determine the server's resilience to rogue software.

2. Here you need to discuss the organisation of UNIX's filing system. Your answer should be put into context by mentioning the fact that, because UNIX is a multi-user operating system, the files of individual users must be protected – unlike, say, Windows or DOS. You must discuss the fact that the directory structure in a UNIX environment is not disk based but directory based, which means that it is not limited to the size or location of a physical disk drive or even a machine. It is always worth using a diagram to illustrate your answer.

3. To answer this question, you need to discuss how filing system security is implemented in UNIX. You need to discuss the fact that filing system security in UNIX centres around the idea of file owner, file group and the rest of the world, and that permissions for access can be granted or revoked from either or all on a controlled basis. You should discuss how such access is granted and, if possible, illustrate your answer with the required commands. Some discussion of how the security may be increased further (using inherited rights) is also extremely worthwhile.

Section 5

Further reading and research

See the *www.PhilipIrving.com* web site for up-to-date further reading and support for this chapter.

Afzal, A. (2002) *UNIX Unbounded: A Beginning Approach*. Prentice Hall. ISBN: 0 13092 836 8. Section 2.

Chapter 9
Setting up a networked operating system

Chapter summary

The correct installation of a networked operating system is critical – NOSs must be very reliable and readily available and a poor setup can jeopardise this. This chapter sets out the basics of the most common tasks involved in setting up a networked operating system:

- Installing and configuring a networked operating system.
- Creating a suitable user environment.
- Managing printer services.

However, there is not the space here to cover everything you need to know to set up and configure a networked operating system; this is meant as a guide only.

Learning outcomes

After studying this chapter you should aim to test your achievement of the following outcomes. You should be able to:

Outcome 1: Installing and configuring Linux and its applications
Understand the steps involved in configuring a typical NOS and in installing an application. Question 1 at the end of this chapter will test you on this.

Outcome 2: Configuring the user environment
Understand the need for, and be able to configure, the end user environment. Question 2 at the end of this chapter will test you on this.

Outcome 3: Printer setup and options
Understand the issues involved with the installation and maintenance of printers. Question 3 at the end of this chapter will test you on this.

How will you be assessed on this?

Assessment in this area is not straightforward. Ideally, an assessor would like to see a student install an operating system successfully. However, pressures of time often mean they are forced to ask students to prepare a guide that will allow anyone to install an operating system. You may also be asked to establish groups, to add users and add these users to groups. You may well be tested on your understanding of this in an exam or TCT.

Section 1

Installing Linux and applications

Networked operating systems (NOS) are complex pieces of software and need careful installation and management. For the purposes of this chapter, Linux's Mandrake Version 9 will be installed. However, this is a general installation guide for Mandrake Linux Version 9.0 – this installation cannot cover every possible user configuration. A PC is one of the most complicated computers available – a trip to a local PC shop will demonstrate the vast range of equipment available (e.g. CD-ROMs, DVDs, scanners, processors, memory, etc.). This vast array of products means that just about every PC is different. This makes the installation of a complex operating system such as Linux difficult – there are so many choices. Whilst this is a general guide, it is strongly recommended you visit Mandrake's website (*www.mandrake.com*) where you will find many installation manuals and a great deal of information about installing Linux. This chapter covers a new and full installation.

> CRUCIAL TIP
>
> Installing Linux can be a very painful experience. One of the best ways of avoiding this is to select a powerful version of Linux that is renowned for its ease of installation. In early 2003, I found Mandrake Version 9 to be the easiest to install.

Installation process

> CRUCIAL TIP
>
> Warning! This process may well destroy applications or data resident on a computer system. Proceed with caution and, preferably, use a machine at university or college that has been allocated for such use.

First steps

Mandrake Version 9 is undoubtedly one of the easiest versions of Linux to install. The best way of installing 9.0 is to enter the BIOS settings of the machine and then set it to boot from the CD. Next, the first installation disk should be inserted into the CD-ROM drive and the machine rebooted (making sure the BIOS settings are saved first!). The initial Mandrake screen appears (Figure 9.1).

Figure 9.1   Initial Mandrake screen

Language selection

Press the enter key to begin the installation. Mandrake installation then begins and you are presented with the language selection screen (Figure 9.2). Notice the process indication on the left-hand side – red is to be done, green is done and amber is current. Language selection is obviously important; it will affect all system documentation.

Figure 9.2   Language selection screen

Licence agreement

You are then presented with the licence agreement which you should accept only if you really do accept it. Figure 9.3 shows a sample screen.

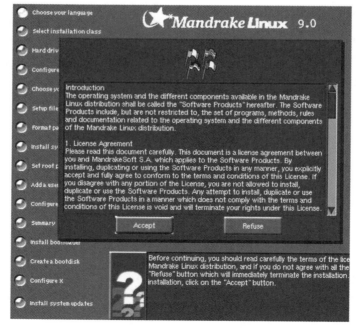

Figure 9.3   Sample screen – licence agreement

Installation class

Next you are asked to select the installation class – default or expert (Figure 9.4). The default installation is acceptable for our purposes so we should accept it. The further choice required in this screen is the type of installation: is it a new installation? An upgrade? An upgrade to packages only? If you select new installation the old installation is almost completely wiped out; upgrade allows you to upgrade the current installation; and update packages allows you to update the packages installed. As this is a new installation, select new.

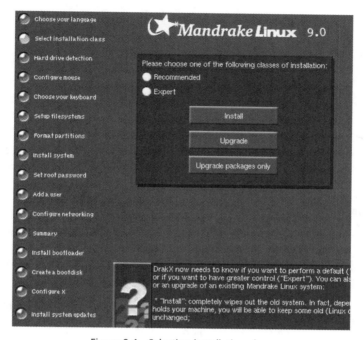

Figure 9.4   Selecting installation class

Mount points

The next part of the installation process asks you to select where Linux is to be installed. It presents you with four options:

- use free space;
- use existing partition;
- use the free space on the Windows partition (if installed);
- erase entire disk.

Again, ensure you wish to proceed with the installation and that your data is backed up. Select 'Use free space'.

Selecting packages

Linux comes with a number of packages that have been grouped together in 9.0. You will be presented with four groups:

- Workstation (if the machine is to be used as a workstation, select the packages you want to be available).
- Development (choose any programming languages you require).
- Server (install the server utilities required).
- Graphical (choose your preferred graphical environment – you must choose at least one).

At this point tool tips will be active so, as you move over each package, a short description of that package should be given. For our purposes select workstation, server and graphical. Within each, select the packages as required by your tutor.

Root password

Root is the superuser of the UNIX system – essentially its God. The root password must be protected and forgetting the password could mean reinstallation of the software. However, the root password must not be written down if at all possible: this would compromise the system. The password is not displayed on the screen and it will be asked for twice.

Adding users

At this point, users can be added to the system. These are ordinary users with ordinary privileges. Ideally, you should create a user for yourself to allow yourself access to the system in a conventional way. Yes, root can provide you with such access but you should avoid using it on a day-to-day basis.

Checking miscellaneous parameters

The installation utility automatically detects just about everything in the system. It now presents this information for verification. The following items should be presented:

- Mouse.
- Keyboard.
- Time zone.
- Printer (if present).
- Sound card (if present).
- TV card (if present).
- ISDN card (if present).

If you disagree with any of the settings , click on the option to alter it. For example, click on 'no printer' to open the printer dialogue configuration. This will allow you to configure the printers. Time is translated from GMT to local time, according to the time zone you select. Linux assumes the system clock to be GMT, and you should unselect this option to let it know local time and the system clock are in the same time zone. Automatic time synchronisation is also possible if you have a working Internet connection.

Configuring X, the graphical server

The graphical server is the heart of the Linux graphical interface upon which all graphical environments (e.g. KDE) are based. At this stage you will be presented with a list of available resolutions and colour depths available for your hardware. Choose the one that best suits your needs (this can be changed later). When you are satisfied with your choice, click on OK. A window will now appear. This asks if you can see what's being displayed. If you can see the message, answer 'yes' to proceed. If not, it will revert to the previous settings after 10 seconds.

Installing updates from the Internet

The Internet is used to distribute newer applications than those on the distribution media and also to provide bug fixes. This section asks if you wish to download these. If you click 'yes', you will be presented with a list of update sites – choose the nearest to you. You will then be presented with a package selection tree. Review the selection and press 'install' to retrieve.

Complete!

Your installation is now complete – simply click on OK to reboot the system.

Installing applications

Further applications can be added after install by inserting the LINX boot CD, rebooting and selecting the 'Upgrade packages option'. Follow the instructions as for installation.

Adding users and groups

Adding users and groups is a relatively straightforward task in Linux. Click on K (bottom left of the screen) and select 'config... Other... Kuser (User Manager)' (Figure 9.5).

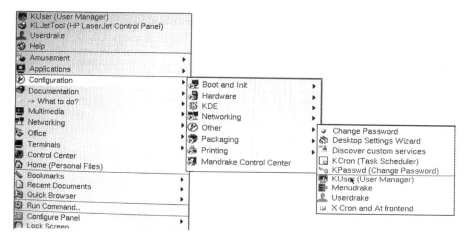

Figure 9.5   Configuring users

You are then presented with the 'add users' screen (Figure 9.6).

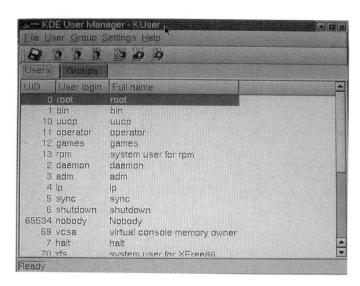

Figure 9.6   Add user screen

Select the users tab and press the add icon (second from the left). In this panel, you can specify user name (Figure 9.7).

Figure 9.7   Adding user

Click on OK. Further details for the user are set in the 'complete all properties' dialogue box (Figure 9.8).

Figure 9.8   Complete all properties dialogue box

The password can be set by clicking 'set password'. To add a group, click on 'add group' from the user configuration screen and select the fifth button. You will be presented with the group configuration screen (Figure 9.9).

Figure 9.9   Group configuration screen

Enter the name of the group and click on OK. The group is now created. Users can be added to the group by returning to the 'complete all properties' section of the user configuration dialogue box and selecting their group membership (Figure 9.10).

Figure 9.10   Selecting group membership

You should select their primary group and any secondary groups required. Deleting users and groups or removing users from groups can be achieved in a similar fashion.

─── CRUCIAL CONCEPT ───

The correct installation of Linux is the key to the success of the operating system. Therefore when installing the operating system, ensure you make the right choices.

Quick test

Briefly outline the steps involved in installing a version of Linux.

Section 2

Configuring the user environment

Once a NOS is installed, the user environment normally needs to be configured. Configuration includes allocating users to a group, giving users access to the facilities of that group, creating login scripts to set the users' environment and, possibly, creating menu scripts to tighten security and to make the system easier to use.

User environment

As standard, UNIX provides two types of user environment – a command line interface (CLI), which is a text-driven interface similar to DOS, and a graphical user interface (GUI) similar to Windows. Which is chosen is a matter of personal choice and environmental conditions. If using a UNIX machine, you will be able to use the GUI but, if working remotely (for example through the Internet), you would use the CLI. Both interfaces will give access to files and will provide the user with full access to the server.

One of the most popular ways of using a UNIX server is to implement Windows as the desktop operating system and to configure it to use UNIX as the server. For files, this can be achieved quite easily by setting Windows to use a remote drive, which should be configured as NFS. NFS (networked file system), as we saw in Chapter 8, allows UNIX to share its filing system over a network. NFS is also available on Windows-based machines. Other applications (such as Oracle), tend to work in one of two ways. The first is as a piece of software installed locally (in the case of Oracle, SQL*Net) that allows applications on the PC to be 'Oracle aware' and to access the database on the server. For example, a list of all students' names and email addresses might be required in an Excel spreadsheet. By using the appropriate software, a query can be built in Excel that will then be sent to the Oracle database on UNIX. The UNIX-based software will then process the query and return the required list into the spreadsheet. In this example, the UNIX machine is behaving as a true server – it is using its immense processing power to retrieve the required data to send to the PC.

The second popular way of accessing a server is through a web-based interface. As web pages and dynamic web pages develop, it is becoming possible to provide end users with an interface to an application that is held centrally on the server. Using the server in this way means an increased load on the server but, at the same time, the PCs need less power. As this technology develops, scripts written in Java will be executable on a PC, thus reducing the server's workload.

User interfaces

GUIs provide the end user with a point-and-click environment in which they can control and run their applications. Multi-user GUIs have extensions that allow them to deal with file access privileges. They also have an interface that permits the management of quite complex activities (providing the user has the rights of access to them), such as adding a user, a group or a device.

The real power of a UNIX server, however, comes in the form of the CLI. In the CLI, commands are submitted to the operating system via a **shell**. A shell is an environment that allows commands to be issued (like DOS), and it also has facilities to control input and output and programming facilities that allow complex sets of actions to be performed. A unique feature of the CLI in UNIX is that there are many to choose from. The user is able to select the shell that best matches his or her experience and current needs. These shells are incredibly powerful and have a programming language of their own. One of the most common and powerful general-purpose shells is the Korn.

As with DOS, it is possible to place commands that would normally be keyed in at the command line into a file. This file can then be given execute permission and executed. Such a file (containing UNIX shell commands) is known as a **script** (or shell script). Executing the script is equivalent to keying in the commands within it. UNIX shells are quite sophisticated programming languages in their own right, and there are entire books devoted to programming in them. Together with the large number of special utility programs provided as standard, scripts make UNIX an extremely powerful operating system: they provide UNIX with an extensive programming language and an extremely flexible environment for controlling and configuring users.

Login scripts

Login scripts are similar to the autoexec.bat and the config.sys files of Windows/DOS except that, in a multi-user environment, they work on a per-user basis rather than on a machine basis. Thus, whenever a user logs on to a UNIX machine, his or her environment is configured automatically. Such things as the preferred editor or printer are set and, in the case of systems that use KDE or CDE graphical desktop environments, the preferred Windows settings are also set. Login scripts in UNIX vary depending upon the shell in use. Each shell has a different startup file, which provides flexibility when configuring the environment. The file's name depends upon the default shell in use – UNIX has different names, one for each shell. The one for the Korn shell is known as .profile (it will be remembered from the last chapter that the . at the front causes the file to be hidden).

Figure 9.11 shows a default .profile script. The lines that begin with a # are comment lines. The fourth line will print the phrase 'Hello Im running .profile' to the screen. Line 5 is interesting. It sets up an alias to allow the user to run the UNIX command ls -lisa by keying in dir. Line 6 sets the working path, and line 7 makes the working path usable. Line 8 sets the type of terminal in use as a virtual terminal (VT) type 100.

```
$ cat .profile|more
#       This is the default standard profile provided to a user.
#       They are expected to edit it to meet their own needs.

echo Hello Im running .profile
alias dir="ls -lisa"
PATH=$OPENWINHOME/bin:$OPENWINHOME/lib:$ORACLE_HOME/lib
export PATH
TERM=vt100;export TERM
```

Figure 9.11   Default .profile script

Menu systems

Often, administrators will want to make the system easy to use and may also want to increase security – if the end users are not allowed access to the operating system commands, they can do a great deal less damage both by accident and maliciously. The script in Figure 9.12 provides the end user with a menu system. The user can choose to get the date, the current directory, a directory listing or can exit. Sample output is shown in Figure 9.13. By inserting a call to this script (together with the UNIX trap command) into the user's .profile file, the administrator is able to control what the user is and is not able to do. The trap command traps break commands (e.g. control-c), which prevents the user from breaking out of the menu. Figure 9.14 shows the revised .profile (including the trap command).

```
$ cat menu
#!/bin/ksh
#Simple menu script written by P J Irving 3/9/02
select REPLY in "System Date" "Current Directory" "Directory Listing" "Exit"
do
    case $REPLY in
        "System Date")
            date
            ;;
        "Current Directory")
            pwd
            ;;
        "Directory Listing")
            ls -l
            ;;
        "Exit")
            break
            ;;
        *)
            echo "I do not recognise your choice"
            ;;
    esac
done
```

Figure 9.12   Simple menu script

```
$ menu
1) System Date
2) Current Directory
3) Directory Listing
4) Exit
#? 1
Tuesday September 9 18:25:31 BST 2002
#? 2
/home/phil/unixbook
#? 3
total 2
-rwx- - - - - - 1 phil staff          354 Apr 27 18:20 menu
#? 8
I do not recognise your choice
1) System Date
2) Current Directory
3) Directory Listing
4) Exit
#? 4
$
```

Figure 9.13   Sample output from the script in Figure 9.12

```
$cat .profile|more
#       This is the default standard profile provided to a user.
#       They are expected to edit it to meet their own needs.

echo Hello Im running .profile
alias dir="ls -lisa"
PATH=$OPENWINHOME/bin:$OPENWINHOME/lib:$ORACLE_HOME/lib
export PATH
TERM=vt100;export TERM
tap 'echo you cant use ctrl=-c' INT
menu
```

Figure 9.14   Revised .profile script (note the trap command)

CRUCIAL CONCEPT

Menus are very useful. They provide the user with limited choice and therefore limited functionality within the system. They are very powerful when combined with login scripts, the break command allowing the user to undertake the tasks on the menu without accessing the operating system. This increases internal security.

Quick test

Briefly outline how shell scripts in the UNIX environment can help to make the server secure.

Section 3

Printer setup and options

NOSs tend to have many different printers that are often located in users' offices . It is important, therefore, that both the printer and the queue are set up correctly and that user output is directed to the correct printer (this is usually done in the user configuration file – see Section 2).

Setting up the printer

Printer installation was covered earlier in this chapter. The following are general points concerning the attachment of printers. Printers can be attached to UNIX systems in a variety of ways: they can be attached directly to the computer system via serial or parallel ports; they can be attached via printer server units networked to the UNIX machine; and some workstations provide for the direct connection of a printer.

When installing a printing device, that device's use must be considered carefully. If the printer is to print on secure stationery (e.g. cheques), it must be secured both physically and logically. Logical security is necessary to remove the threat of someone printing his or her own cheque. Indeed, if a printer contains anything other than blank paper it will probably need to be controlled. Pre-printed order forms could be open to fraudulent use, as could invoices, credit notes, etc. Even letter-headed stationery needs to be protected in some way – it is relatively expensive and can be wasted if used for program listings, etc.

In general, printers are found in the /dev directory and have the following attributes:

Device name	Description
/dev/lp0	First parallel printer
/dev/lp1	Second parallel printer
/dev/lp2	Third parallel printer

Serial printers are assigned to serial devices (for example, /dev/ttyS0 for the first serial printer, /dev/ttyS1 for the second, and so on).

Printing options

To support multi-user access, printer functions are extended in UNIX. The basic print command is lp or lpr (an abbreviation for line printer), followed by the filename (e.g. lp <myfile> would queue the file myfile for later printing). Often users wish to check the status of printing, perhaps to determine the position of their print job in the queue. This can be achieved using the lpq command. When using the lpq command, each entity in the queue has a unique job number. Should a user wish to remove a job from the queue, he or she needs to know this job number (see below).

It is usual for a multi-user system to have several printers connected to it and, providing he or she has permission, the user can select whichever printer he or she wishes to use for a job. This is achieved by using the –P switch in the lp command. Thus lp –P <printer> <filename> will cause the file named to be printed on the printer named. Status check and job cancellation also support the –P switch.

Managing printer queues

In most cases, all printers can be seen and managed by the systems administrator. Printers in UNIX usually need little management other than 'standard' maintenance (toner, ribbons, paper, etc.). Occasionally, jobs need to be removed from the print queue, which can be done by a user (providing he or she owns the job). System administrator privilege is only necessary when the owner of a job is not available and his or her job requires attention. Table 9.1 provides a summary of printer maintenance commands.

Table 9.1   Printer maintenance commands

Command	Description	Example
lpstat printer	Displays information about the current status of the LP print service	lpstat –o all
lpq	Displays the status of jobs on the printer specified	lpq –p stuprinter
lprm	Cancels printing of the specified job	lprm 123

The lpq, if used without any parameters, displays information about the default printer's queue. When used with the −P switch this allows a particular printer name to be specified, and it provides the following information:

- Print job ID.
- The owner of the job.
- The name of the file being printed.
- The size of the file.

The lprm can be used to remove jobs from the print queue. Again, the default printer's queue will be accessed unless another printer name is specified. There are two ways of using the lprm command – to remove specified jobs from the queue or to remove all jobs from the queue.

To remove particular files, the job's ID must be established (using the lpq command). To remove job 321, lprm 321 would be keyed in. Care must be taken when typing lprm as lprm on its own will remove all the jobs from the default printer's queues. To remove jobs from a specific printer queue, lprm -queuename should be used, where queuename is the name of the queue to be cleared.

Many variants of UNIX have specific commands for printer management (for instance, IBM/HP/SCO/Solaris, etc., use lpadmin for the general administration of printers and cancel for cancelling print jobs).

CRUCIAL CONCEPT

Managing printers in Linux means being responsible not only for your own work but also for that of others. Print queues allow users to send their jobs for printing where they will queue until it is their turn on the printer.

CRUCIAL TIP

Most of these commands have GUI equivalents.

Quick test

Briefly discuss how print jobs are managed, using the command line in Linux.

Section 4

End of chapter assessment

Questions

1. Outline the major steps involved in installing Linux.

2. Figure 9.15 shows a shell script. Briefly discuss what the shell script does, annotating this example with appropriate comments, and provide a sample output. Discuss why such scripts are very useful for security.

```
$ cat menu
#!/bin/ksh

select REPLY in "System Date" "Current Directory" "Directory Listing" "Exit"
do
  case $REPLY in
    "System Date")
        date
        ;;
    "Current Directory")
        pwd
        ;;
    "Directory Listing")
        ls -l
```

```
            ;;
      "Exit")
            break
            ;;
      *)
            echo "I do not recognise your choice"
            ;;
      esac
done
```

Figure 9.15   Sample shell script

3. Briefly discuss how printers are managed in the UNIX operating system

Answers

1. To be fair, such a question is unlikely in an exam or TCT. You are far more likely to be asked either to install a version of Linux or to produce a user guide on the installation of Linux. In the latter case, you should note your intended audience and ensure that the language and style used are appropriate for this audience. Ultimately, the assessors are seeking to establish whether you can install a multi-user operating system, and the production of a manual gives them something that can be handed to the external examiner as proof of your abilities.

2. Rather than being cruel and asking you to write a shell script in an exam or TCT, the assessor will often give you a shell script and ask you to annotate it with comments and give a sample output. This is a less painful way of ensuring you understand scripts. In this case, the script is a menu system that allows the user to call on a number of utilities. When it is executed it will present the output shown in Figure 9.16. You should annotate the shell script with appropriate comments. Remember, the assessor is not looking for comments such as 'this line prints out'; he or she is looking for a deeper understanding – for example, 'this section of the script traps and processes an invalid user input'. Finally, you need to identify why menus are so important to security in an operating system. Your answer to this question should ideally include the trap command being used in the shell's startup file.

```
$ menu
1) System Date
2) Current Directory
3) Directory Listing
4) Exit
#? 1
Tuesday September 9 18:25:31 BST 2002
#? 2
/home/phil/unixbook
#? 3
total 2
-rwx- - - - - - 1 phil staff 354 Apr 27 18:20 menu
#? 8
I do not recognise your choice
1) System Date
2) Current Directory
3) Directory Listing
4) Exit
#? 4
```

Figure 9.16   Sample output from question 2

3. To answer this question you need to need to highlight the issues associated with printer management, list the commands used for printer management, discuss the function of each command and give an appropriate example of each command's use.

Section 5

Further reading and research

See the *www.PhilipIrving.com* website for up-to-date further reading and support for this chapter.

Afzal, A. (2002) *UNIX Unbounded: A Beginning Approach*. Prentice Hall ISBN: 0 13092 736 8. Section 2.

Dick, D. (2002) *PC Support Handbook*. Dumbreck Publishing. ISBN: 0 95417 110 1. UNIX chapter.

For man commands in Unix, see *www.mandrake.com* (accessed July 2003).

Chapter 10
Network management

Chapter summary

Managing a network is extremely important. There is a myth that once a network is installed it will virtually run itself. For all but the very simplest of networks, this is simply not the case. Today's networks are highly complex and often mission critical to organisations: they cannot be treated piecemeal – to perform well they must be managed and managed well. This chapter provides an introduction to network management. Of all management tasks, it is the backup that is the most important. This is reflected in its treatment in this chapter.

Learning outcomes

After studying this chapter you should aim to test your achievement of the following outcomes. You should be able to:

Outcome 1: Creating users and groups
Create users and groups and understand the security implications. Question 1 at the end of this chapter will test you on this.

Outcome 2: Managing networks
Understand how to manage networks in a proactive fashion to provide high-availability. Question 2 at the end of this chapter will test you on this.

Outcome 3: Security
Understand the need for network and system security, be able to evaluate security and devise, implement and monitor security policies. Question 3 at the end of this chapter will test you on this.

How will you be assessed on this?

The subject matter of this chapter is a blend of both practice and theory (although the theory is very practically focused!) and is likely to be assessed as such. As time is often tight in modules and resources are limited, it is likely your assessor will ask you to write a user manual detailing how to undertake the practical aspects. Such topics as backup and security lend themselves very well to exams and TCTs.

Section 1

Creating users and groups

One of the most common breaches of security in NOS is the creation of fictitious user and group accounts through which fraudulent transactions can be made.

Therefore, whilst this section deals with the process of creating users and groups, it also outlines the management procedures necessary to maintain security.

Creating users and groups

When establishing a UNIX system for the first time, careful consideration must be given to groups and their members. Most organisations have distinct groups (e.g. human resources, finance, manufacturing, etc.) that would naturally form UNIX groups. However, the nature of the information stored on the system dictates that groups must be selected carefully. For instance, not everyone in finance should have access to the printer containing cheques and, if everyone has access to the purchase order system, fraudulent purchase orders or invoices could be created. Thus user needs should be discussed carefully and user IDs should be created in an accountable and controlled fashion. Control issues are usually dealt with by the human resources manager or head of the relevant department, and these people should detail the access levels required clearly. System administrators should grant only the minimum access necessary.

Similarly, when employees leave a company, the human resources department needs to inform the systems administrator, who should then suspend the user account. All memos sent by the human resources department should be kept by the systems administrator as confirmation for audit purposes. The accounts should be suspended rather than deleted, which leaves a trail for subsequent system auditing. Any changes to user accounts also need to have an audit trail. For example, if the head of purchasing wants a user to have access to the purchase order system, a memo should be sent to the systems administrator asking for this to be done. Simply acting on verbal information could place the administrator in a precarious position if there was a fraudulent incident.

This type of user management varies according to the organisation. For example, universities manage huge numbers of accounts for both staff and students. At the end of each academic year, roughly one third of all student accounts will cease and, at the beginning of the academic year, a new batch of accounts will be created. At the University of Sunderland there are approximately 15 000 students requiring approximately 5000 accounts to be created each September.

Different methods can be used to automate the creation of accounts, particularly in UNIX, but the accounts must still be created in a controlled way. Accounts represent the basic level of access to the network and the computer system. One possible solution for a university is to create user accounts from the registration system – a file could be downloaded from the registration system and processed via UNIX scripts to create an account. As each student in the registration system is a valid student, this process is safe. Standard student rights would also be given, as would standard passwords – perhaps a date of birth or some other code the students choose at the time of registration.

CRUCIAL CONCEPT

Control must be exercised over the creation of users. Creating users in an ad hoc fashion may well compromise the system.

Management of users

Once the process of creating accounts is complete, administrators need to be aware that a higher workload will follow from the increased number of users. Management of users, therefore, tends to fall into one of two categories:

- Normal user management.
- Exceptional user management.

Normal users are the users systems administrators would expect to deal with each day – requests for help with a forgotten password, more disk storage space, printer problems, etc. Obviously, the higher the number of users, the higher the workload from this category of users. As its name suggests, exceptional user management involves dealing with exceptional cases, and these might mean breaches of security. The network manager or systems administrator should be on the lookout for security breaches and should investigate accordingly. Security breaches can often be detected as long continuous logins, and perhaps the user doesn't log out when leaving for lunch or in the evening. Logins after hours or from strange or unknown computers often indicate a security breach. Ideally, of course, this should be blocked by the organisation's security policy. Most operating systems have extensive facilities for monitoring security and for tracking users. For example, the who command in UNIX can show who is currently logged on to the system, whereas the last command gives details of previous logins. Although primitive tools, they are a useful starting point for tracking users and monitoring security.

The management of workgroups also tends to be exceptional. Occasionally a user will be assigned to another workgroup, either alongside his or her current group or as a full transfer. Systems administrators need to ensure users are allocated to the correct groups using the chgrp command (see Chapter 8).

CRUCIAL CONCEPT

Users must be managed to keep the system healthy. Security is dependent upon good user management.

Quick test

Briefly discuss the issues involved in user management.

Section 2

Managing networks

As has been noted elsewhere, the installation of a network is only the beginning: the successful management of a network is paramount if it is to be a valuable asset to an organisation. Key tasks in managing a network are ensuring continuity and integrity through backups and ensuring continued functionality through the continuous monitoring of resource usage.

Estimating resource usage

Estimating resource usage is an important part of network management. The goals of such management are to detect trends arising from the use of the network and to use these trends to plan future upgrades. To identify trends accurately and to provide a benchmark for resolving problems, it is important to measure the network and its performance immediately after installation. Known as baselining, this process ideally measures the load on the network and the network's response time at each user's machine. Only when this information has been collected can meaningful comparisons be made if users complain of the network's performance.

CRUCIAL TIP

The system must be baselined. If not, there will be nothing to measure current performance against.

Other measurements that should be taken include disk usage and the disk filing system. These can be taken using the following commands:

- df
- du

df provides information on used and available disk space (in kilobytes), as shown in Figure 10.1; du provides information on the number of kilobytes allocated to each of the specified filenames, as shown in Figure 10.2.

```
$ df
Filesystem    kybytes    used      avail      capacity    Mounted on
/dev/staff1    17415     10900     6515       62%         /
/dev/staff2    20300     11000     9300       54%         /usr
```

Figure 10.1 Sample df output

```
$ du|more
2       ./.wastebasket
16      ./.cetables
2       ./.logs
2       ./.tt
46      ./sql/osaass
236     ./sql
2       ./.netscape/cache
264     ./.netscape
2       ./bupdir
6       ./copydir
6       ./BUPDIR
16      ./mydir
6       ./COPYDIR
130     ./Java
2       ./bin
1026    ./soar6
-More-
```

Figure 10.2 Sample du output

Both these commands provide essential information on the filing system. Should the filing system become full, serious problems will arise. This is particularly true if /tmp becomes full as all UNIX applications use this as a 'scratch' area. Careful monitoring of the system is essential if problems are to be avoided, and can only be undertaken if there is a baseline to measure from. The /tmp directory normally only contains temporary files and it is the only directory from which the administrator can safely delete files – other directories contain essential system files and should not be deleted. Applications also usually have directories that grow – for instance, an accounting package will have a directory that contains audit trails. The size of this directory will grow as each transaction is made in the accounting package. The systems administrator should ensure these directories have enough space for their required growth, but the administrator of the accounts package should ensure this directory is maintained and unnecessary files removed.

Measurements should be taken frequently and be recorded. The exact frequency depends upon the machine's usage and the disk quotas imposed on users, but once a week is normally sufficient. Measurements and backups must be taken immediately prior to any software installation or maintenance. It must be remembered that UNIX is a multi-user operating system and, as such, the responsibility for the maintenance of the filing system should be the responsibility of all who use it. The systems administrator should not interfere with user accounts unless a problem is encountered. Instead, the users should be made responsible for the maintenance of their own filing system. This means the users must be trained in the maintenance of filing systems and they must be encouraged to undertake such maintenance. Systems administrators can set a disk quota for each user, that limits the storage space they have available. Setting a 'reasonable' quota is essential as it enforces maintenance discipline in the users and protects the system from large increases in stored data.

CRUCIAL CONCEPT

It is important to monitor the networked system to ensure it continues to meet the organisation's needs.

Managing systems: backup

Perhaps the single most important task in managing any computer system is providing for its continuity. This involves protecting the organisation's data – most organisations cannot survive without access to it, and the following five ways of protecting data are frequently recommended:

- backup
- backup
- backup
- backup
- backup

This is not a misprint – it is intentional. Users and systems administrators must realise that the only way an organisation can retrieve lost data is if it was backed up in the first place. Without a backup there is little chance of an organisation being able to retrieve its data. When it can, this is often very expensive and takes a long time. Data is the lifeblood of an organisation and, if it is starved of its data, it is unlikely it will be able to survive uninjured. If the data loss were complete, the organisation would probably not survive. Consider a credit card company that lost all its customers' balances – it would probably never be able to recoup all money it was owed. If a bank had major problems and lost the balance of its customers' accounts, how would their customers react?

It should also be understood that most systems change on a frequent basis – especially the data. As such, regular backups should be taken and the organisation should be prepared to lose any data that isn't backed up. The organisation should ask itself how much data it is prepared to lose – if the answer is very little, regular backups must be taken. Backups cannot be undertaken piecemeal: they are essential to the well-being of the organisation. As such it should be made someone's responsibility, on his or her job description, to take regular backups, and someone else's responsibility to ensure they are taking place. If not, they may not happen, which could result in catastrophe. Backups must be planned and a set of 'idiot-proof' instructions produced to ensure everyone understands how to take a backup.

Backup now complete, what next?

It is no good simply backing up a computer and trusting the backup has worked. The backup needs to be tested to ensure the data has been copied. The tape's test needs to be thorough – a backup is only as good as its test. Occasionally, someone will take a tape listing from the backup tape to verify something has been written. However, on most tapes the backup directory is at the very front of the tape and the directory may well have been written but nothing else. The only way a backup can be truly tested is to restore all the files.

Unless the organisation has a separate computer with the same version of the operating system installed, this is usually not possible and an alternative must be found. However, the files should never be restored on to the same computer – if the backup has failed the original files will be corrupted.

If the organisation does not have a 'spare' computer, it is best to write a script that places a copy of a master text file around the filing system in predetermined locations (usually around mission critical data – both before and after it). The backup should then be taken and these text files removed from the computer. An attempt should then be made to restore the files from the backup and compare them to the master. If the copies verify OK there is a high probability the backup will be OK. If not, another backup should be made immediately on another tape.

Backups can be made easily on UNIX using either the tar or cpio commands. The tar command normally has the following syntax:

tar –cvf /dev/rmt0	for backup
tar –tvf /dev/rmt0	for tape listing
tar –xvf /dev/rmt0	for the extraction of files.

Figure 10.3 shows tar being used to create a backup, to list the contents of the backup and, finally, to restore two files.

```
$
$ tar -cvf backdir/up/bup date*.*
a date.txt 1K
a date2.txt 1K
$
$ tar -tvf backdir/bup
tar: blocksize=6
-rw-r-r- 1069/10      34 Apr 26 11:34 1999 date.txt
-rw- - - - - -1069/10   34 Apr 26 11:34 1999 date2.txt
$rm da*.*
$is–l da*.*
da*.*:No such file or directory
$tar =xvf backdir/bup date.txt
ta: blocksize=6
x date.txt, 34 bytes, 1 tape blocks
$ tar -xvf backdir/bup date 2.txt
tar: blocksize=6
x date2.txt, 34 bytes, 1 tape blocks
$
```

Figure 10.3   Sample tar output

Further details can be obtained from the manual entries of tar. Users should be wary that tar could corrupt certain types of files (only the backup copy is corrupt). These include ORACLE databases, which must either be exported (an ORACLE command) prior to backup or must be backed up using cpio (which does not corrupt).

―――――――――――― CRUCIAL CONCEPT ――――――――――
Backups must be tested regularly to prove the data can be restored.

Types of backup

There are three main backup techniques, and the selection of the most appropriate technique is just as important as selecting the right backup device.

Full

Performing a full backup on a frequent basis is usually the best way of protecting the system. This involves taking a copy of all the data, applications and systems files (including the operating system) and storing these to tape. Everything on the system is copied to tape, which requires a backup device with a large storage capacity. Because of the volume of information being stored, this type of backup takes the longest to perform. Should the organisation need 24-hour access to its data, this kind of backup can be disruptive. However, because all the information is on one backup set, this type of backup is the quickest way of restoring the system.

Full backups are perhaps easiest in UNIX and can be achieved simply by using the standard tar command: tar –cvf /dev/rmt0.

Incremental

Incremental backups are used to cut down the time taken for a full backup. Using this method, a full backup is taken and then the first incremental backup copies only the files modified (be they system or data files) since the full backup. The second incremental backup copies only those files (system or data) modified since the first incremental backup, and so on. This drastically cuts down on the time taken to back up but can lead to a complex chain of tapes as each tape contains only files modified since the last backup. This means it would take a lot longer to restore the files and that the backup is dependent upon more tapes, which increases the probability of failure.

To make an incremental backup in UNIX, we need to 'find' the appropriate files and use this list to perform the backup. The find command in UNIX finds all the files that have been modified today: find / -mtime –1 ! –type d –print. This command will find all files starting from the root directory (/). The ! means not and the –type d means directory. Thus it will not find directories, as not everything in the directory will have changed.

UNIX permits command substitution, which allows a user to use a command in place of a string or a variable. This is achieved using the ' quotes, usually located at the top left of the keyboard. Thus the above command can be incorporated into the tar command: tar -cvf / dev/rmt0 ' find / -mtime -1 ! -type d -print'.

Differential

Differential backup is really a compromise between the previous two backup techniques. With differential backup, a full backup is taken and then subsequent differential backups. Each differential backup copies all files modified since the **last full backup**. This affords a higher level of protection than incremental backups but not as high as a full backup. It also takes longer to back up than an incremental backup but less time than a full backup. Finally, it takes longer to restore than a full backup but not as long as an incremental backup.

Differential backups in UNIX require a slightly different version of the find command. When the full backup is taken, the systems administrator creates a file (e.g. /tmp/lastbackup) that would have the date and time of the backup contained within it. The above command could then be modified to search for files that are newer than this: tar -cvf /dev/rmt0 ' find . -newer /tmp/lastbackup ! –type d -print'. Thus all the files that have been modified since the date of the /tmp/lastbackup file will be archived. The date and time of the /tmp/ lastbackup file can be easily modified using the touch command: touch /tmp/lastbackup.

CRUCIAL CONCEPT

The time taken to restore is of the utmost importance – this is the time when you need the greatest speed. Fast backups are also important – normal business should not be interfered with. Therefore full backups are always recommended unless there are compelling reasons not to do so.

Backup cycles

Introduction

Tapes must be used in accordance with the manufacturer's guidelines (in terms of heat, humidity and acclimatisation) and should also be cycled. The manufacturers issue instructions with tapes detailing constraints on their use which must be adhered to. The cycling of tapes is of the utmost importance – each tape should be used frequently and to a similar extent. Tapes stretch as they are used, especially at first. If they are underused, reliability may be impaired just as if they are overused. Systems administrators should ensure each tape is used a similar number of times. This cannot be achieved by random selection. Therefore two cycling techniques are discussed below that allow for the efficient cycling of tapes (the second affords a high level of protection, assuming a full backup is taken every night).

Grandfather/father/son

This is perhaps one of the simplest yet most effective backup cycles. The first tape created becomes the son and is kept. The second tape created becomes the new son, the older one becoming the father. When the third tape is used, this becomes the son, the oldest tape becomes the grandfather and the previous son becomes the father.

Thus there is a whole generation of backup tapes and it is possible to recover back to the third backup. In a daily cycle, this means that files lost up to three days ago can be recovered. As computer systems become larger with more users, lost files are often not noticed in three days. For example, consider a part-time class at a university – they may only be in once a week. If they discover a lost file, it is too late to recover it using this method of cycling. Thus organisations have adopted more complex strategies for cycling.

Four-week cycle

This method preserves each week's backups for a further four weeks. Full backups are taken on separate tape sets every business day. The last working day's tape is kept and the remainder are reused. This pattern is repeated for week two to week four. In week five, the first weekly backup tape is brought back into service. Assuming all data can be fitted on to one cartridge and assuming five working days, this requires 24 cartridges. However, the weekly tapes should not be used solely for weekly backups – this would underuse them and so they could fail.

CRUCIAL TIP

Backups should be kept for a 'reasonable' time. The definition of reasonable will depend upon the organisation.

Additional considerations

The following should also be considered when undertaking backups:

- Replace tapes regularly (the purchase date should be written on the tape, together with a tally of the number of times used).
- Upon receiving any errors, the tape should be replaced immediately.

- Clean the drive regularly, following the manufacturer's instructions.
- Always store tapes offsite in a fireproof safe.

Quick test

Discuss the major management issues a systems administrator should attend to.

Section 3

Security

Introduction

Computer security is a major issue in computing and not without reason. Most organisations are critically dependent upon their information, and the only copy of this is almost certainly held on computer. The theft of information is serious but even more serious is the organisation being denied access to its own information. Known as a 'denial of service attack', this assault may be as simple as someone accessing the organisation's computer system and changing all the passwords.

The main threats to a computer system are:

- computer misuse;
- attacks on the network;
- computer viruses;
- a disaster of some kind (fire, flood, etc.);
- data loss;
- theft of hardware.

To be effective, security must be based on a sound policy. This policy can then be implemented using a variety of techniques, such as manual procedures, limiting end-user access, firewalls, routers and leased communication lines. This section briefly explores the main issues involved in computer security and provides suggestions to counteract such security problems.

The most important thing an organisation must do to protect itself is to take regular backups. Whilst this will not help prevent attacks on the computer system, it will provide the organisation with a way of recovering its systems should anything happen.

Misuse of computer systems

Computer security is difficult to pin down – many organisations that have experienced security breaches prefer to cover this up as public exposure could cause even more damage. Consider a bank that lost £2 million through poor computer security – would you be happy banking with them? Numerous surveys have shown that as much as two thirds of all computer misuse is committed by employees of the organisations concerned. Common forms of misuse include creating (and paying) bogus employees, creating dummy purchase orders and paying false invoices, etc. Policies therefore need to be in place that make it more difficult for such activities to occur. For example, physically separating duties would make fraud more difficult: the person who pays the invoices should not be the person who creates the purchase order. Similarly, before an employee is added to the payroll, a request to do so must be received from the human resources department. In a similar way, employees must be educated not to share their user IDs and passwords. Someone using your ID or password is effectively you to all system audit trails. Should some form of fraud take place, it is you who will be accused.

Employees who exceed their level of security can also be a problem. Assuming passwords are not shared, the best way to tackle this problem is to configure the user interface. For example, if the user's duties only involve paying invoices, menu systems should be created (see Chapter 9) that offer this option only. It will hence become very difficult for the user to exceed his or her level of authority.

Attacks on the network

Surveys by the Computer Security Institute (CSI) found that 70% of organisations said their network security defences had been breached. Some 60% said that such incidents came from within the organisation itself. Again, the internal threat is greater than the external threat.

Four types of network threat can be identified:

- unstructured
- structured
- external
- internal.

Unstructured threats are mainly in the form of inexperienced individuals using tools they downloaded from the Internet. Whilst not very technically competent, these individuals have some sort of intention or they wouldn't be 'having a go' in the first place. The fact they exist is a problem. Structured threats are from seasoned hackers who are competent and motivated. They have an understanding of networking and more sophisticated tools. External threats are as would be expected, from outside the organisation. Access is secured through dial-up connections or the Internet. Internal threats occur when someone has authorised access to the network or physical access to the networking devices. The physical security of devices and the major cabling is of paramount importance – if someone can physically access your devices, they can probably defeat the passwords (most equipment provides for password recovery from physical access). Similarly, if someone has access to the major cabling simply cutting it will cause a great deal of harm.

Types of attack

There are, broadly, three types of network attack:

- reconnaissance
- access
- denial of service (DoS).

Reconnaissance attacks are like a burglar checking out a neighbourhood – looking for unlocked doors, half-open windows, etc. The burglar doesn't intend to carry out a burglary immediately but is looking for weaknesses. Networks have similar weaknesses. Hackers are looking for folders that are being shared in Windows and that have not been closed, exposed UNIX directories, etc. They will make a note of these weaknesses and come back to exploit them when no one is looking.

Access refers to unauthorised data manipulation, systems access or privilege escalation. Data manipulation occurs when someone views information he or she is not meant to have access to (this could include copying or moving the information). Seasoned hackers will use tools to gain access to this information: just as burglars use lock picks, hackers use password crack or other utilities that either exploit a weakness in the system or simply employ brute force (a tirade of passwords) to gain access. Access attacks that involve privilege escalation are those where a legitimate user (or a hacker who has succeeded in getting low-level access to the system) attempts to gain higher-level access. This can involve running some kind of software – perhaps a password-sniffing tool to identify passwords sent across the network. Shared machines at universities and colleges are particularly prone to this kind of attack.

Denial of service (DoS) attacks are one of the most feared forms. Here the intruder wants to deny an organisation access to its own network or services. In doing so, the intruder prevents that organisation from functioning, and the longer it can be prevented from functioning, the less likely it is it will recover.

CRUCIAL CONCEPT

There are many threats to the network system, the majority coming from within the organisation itself. Systems administrators need to be aware of these threats and be on the lookout for them.

Elements of good practice

It is important that network security is seen as a continuous process: new threats emerge daily so network security must be tested regularly to determine its effectiveness. Figure 10.4 shows the four essential steps in network security.

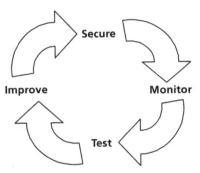

Figure 10.4   Major processes in network security

In the first instance, an organisation needs to identify its security objectives and the resources to be protected. By using network maps, an effective security policy can be devised. This policy can then be implemented (the secure part of Figure 10.4) using such security devices as firewalls, access control lists on a router and encryption and authentication utilities. A firewall is basically a piece of software that filters packets flowing around the network. If the packet is allowable, the filter will allow it to pass; if not, it will be blocked. Obviously, this filter is configurable.

Once the security policy has been implemented, the network needs to be monitored for access breaches or attacks. Commercial software is available for this, such as the Cisco Secure Intrusion Detection System. This software will help to determine whether the network devices have been configured properly. The effectiveness of the safeguards that have been put in place must be tested against the security procedures the organisation has devised. An organisation may have created the best security policy in the world but, unless it is tested, no one will know whether it is working or not. Again, software is available for this (for example, Cisco's Security Scanner).

Finally, security must be improved. This can only be done by collecting and analysing information that has been gathered from the monitoring and testing phases. New vulnerabilities appear every day. Security is a continuous process. The four steps involved should be repeated continuously and, where necessary, amendments to the security policy should be made.

CRUCIAL CONCEPT

Computer security is a continuous process of secure–monitor–test–improve. It cannot be regarded as a one-off measure.

Virus protection

Computer viruses are yet another threat to networks and systems availability. Unfortunately, the development of networks and emails means they can be spread more quickly than they could by floppy disks. The security policy must deal with the threat of computer viruses, which can lead either to a denial of service or can be used to open a 'back door' into the system. With viruses, prevention is definitely better than cure. Protecting the system from viruses involves educating the end users in the need to be aware of the risks of computer viruses and how they are spread, etc. The organisation's policy must aim to minimise the threat of viruses, and the users must work to this policy, either by choice or by force – but the former is more acceptable! Such a policy must:

- regulate the use of floppy disks and CD-ROMs in the organisation;
- control the sending and receiving of email attachments;
- control downloads from the web;
- control the installation of software;
- ensure that every machine has an up-to-date virus checker installed;
- ensure that each machine is regularly updated with the latest version of the anti-virus software.

Users should be discouraged from using CD-ROMs or floppy disks unless they can demonstrate a need and they have been virus checked. Some organisations make unauthorised use a disciplinary offence. Sending and, particularly, receiving email attachments should be discouraged unless absolutely necessary. Even when necessary, these attachments should be in a zipped form rather than executable. This facilitates easier virus checking on the receiving machine. Remember, plain ASCII text is always safe – it is the attachments, etc., that cause the problems. Downloads from the web are extremely dangerous and users should be discouraged from downloading (and certainly installing) software and files. Indeed, the only software that can be safely installed is shrink-wrapped software from a trusted manufacturer or supplier. Each machine should have a reputable, up-to-date virus checker installed, and this must be kept up to date with the latest releases from the manufacturer.

The network operating system also needs to be chosen carefully. A system that offers a high degree of security (with separate logins for each user) and administration rights to the administrator only, will go a long way to protecting itself. Should a virus somehow sneak in to the system, under such conditions it should not be able to infect easily either other users' files or the operating system itself. Regular system backups must be taken and several generations should be kept – restoring yesterday's infected file is of little use but last week's out-of-date uninfected file is of use. These backups should be on external media that can be removed from the system and stored safely. Again, the anti-virus policy must be continuously monitored and updated if it is to remain effective.

CRUCIAL CONCEPT

Viruses are a real threat to organisations. Good administration is essential to minimise this threat.

Quick test

Briefly outline the major items that should be covered in an organisation's security and anti-virus policy.

Section 4

End of chapter assessment

Questions

1. Discuss the major steps involved in creating users and groups in the UNIX operating system. You should pay particular attention to such issues as policy.

2. Briefly discuss the major tasks involved in managing a network and the importance of these tasks.

3. Explain why network security is of the utmost importance and discuss those things considered to be good practice in network security.

Answers

1. This question is in two parts. The first asks you to discuss the major steps involved in creating users and groups on a UNIX system. The second is interested in the control of that creation. For the first part, you need to discuss how an account is created on a UNIX system, outlining the various steps needed to create the account, the group and to allocate the user to a group. For the second part, you should discuss the possible security implications of creating a user or a group and adding/deleting users from that group. Your answer should ideally mention the fact that a user ID is the key to accessing the system and that unauthorised accounts could compromise systems security. You should discuss the need for (and outline), an administrative process that would create accounts/ groups and allocate users to those groups in a secure manner.

2. To answer this question, you need to identify the major tasks involved in managing a network. For each task, you need to discuss briefly the task and its importance in aiding the smooth operation of the network. In the case of more specific tasks, such as backups, you should briefly discuss the various options available and, if possible, outline any advice you would give converning the best methods to back up systems and data.

3. Computer security is of paramount importance and is a cause for concern for most organisations, and your answer should highlight this fact. You should briefly mention the possible threats before going on to outline the elements of good practice. I would recommend you draw the 'security wheel' given in this chapter and discuss each of the steps in detail. It is important that you highlight that computer security is a continuous process and that it must be treated as such – don't forget that new threats appear almost daily.

Section 5

Further reading and research

See the *www.PhilipIrving.com* website for up-to-date further reading and support for this chapter.

Afzal, A. (2002) *UNIX Unbounded: A Beginning Approach*. Prentice Hall . ISBN 0 13092 736 8. Section 2.

Dick, D. (2002) *PC Support Handbook*. Dumbreck Publishing. ISBN: 0 95417 110 1.

Cisco Networking Academy Program (2001) *Second Year Companion Guide*, (2nd edn). Cisco Press. ISBN: 1 58713 029 7. Chapters 8 and 28.

For man commands in Unix, see *www.mandrake.com* (accessed July 2003).

Chapter 11
Connecting to the outside world

Chapter summary

This chapter provides an overview of networking by illustrating how all the equipment works together in order to provide connectivity. Since the Internet is a hot topic at the moment, it outlines how a request for a web page is generated on a PC and handled by the network.

Learning outcomes

After studying this chapter you should aim to test your achievement of the following outcomes. You should be able to:

Outcome 1: Types of Internet connections
Understand the differences between the main types of Internet connections and be able to select the most appropriate for a particular situation. Question 1 at the end of this chapter will test you on this.

Outcome 2: The Internet (TCP/IP) case study
Understand how the Internet operates when requesting and receiving web pages. Question 2 at the end of this chapter will test you on this.

How will you be assessed on this?

Knowing how connection to the Internet and how data travels in the form packets and frames (crossing internal networks and the Internet) will give you the 'big picture' of how networks operate. Even if this is not assessed directly, it will deepen your understanding, which will come through in any assessment you undertake. In a practical assessment, you could be asked to recommend an Internet connection for a given company. You could also be asked in an exam to discuss how connection to the Internet can be achieved and how data is exchanged. You can, of course, weave the content of this chapter into most of your answers for extra marks.

Section 1

Types of Internet connections

Currently there are only two possible ways to connect to the Internet: dial-up lines and local area networks. For the purposes of this chapter, ADSL and cable are considered to be LAN connections, although the chapter does explain briefly how ADSL and cable work.

Dial-up connection

Most people are familiar with this method of connecting to the Internet and it is still by far the most popular, with more than 50% of users still connecting in this fashion. Dial-up connection involves the use of a pair of modems and a telephone line. The modems convert the digital computer signals into analogue signals that are suitable for transmission over the telephone network. Another modem at the other end converts them back. This is known as a point-to-point (PPP) serial link and is available through virtually all ISPs. Once at the ISP's premises, the data is transferred on to its LAN and begins its journey to the Internet. Dial-up connection is also known as plain old telephone service or POTS for short. Typically, modems provide 33.6 K upload speed and 56.6 K download speed.

CRUCIAL TIP

All 56 K modems provide an upload speed of only 33.6 K. This is because this speed is the fastest digital-to-analogue conversion can reliably operate at. The reason the download speed is quicker is because the V.90 standard treats the incoming signal as digital (even though it is analogue) and, therefore, the conversion rule doesn't apply.

ADSL

Asymmetric digital subscriber line (ASDL) is a method by which a permanent connection to the Internet can be provided to an end subscriber using existing telephone lines. Quite simply, this is achieved by dividing the bandwidth of the conventional telephone line into channels, in a similar way that the bandwidth of TV/radio broadcasts is divided into channels (BBC1, BBC2, ITV, etc.) (see Figure 11.1). Technically, this is known as Frequency Division Multiplexing (FDM). Frequency ranges are allocated to particular services. In the case of ADSL, a small frequency range is allocated to the telephone service, a second, larger frequency range to the upstream connection to the Internet and the third, and largest channel to the downstream link to the Internet. Connection requires a device to split the channels (often called a **microfilter**) and, possibly, a broadband modem. The computer and telephone can then attach to the microfilter.

Figure 11.1 ADSL channels

Although the theory sounds straightforward, the cable and equipment that carry ADSL were never meant for this purpose, and so the technology that makes this possible is nothing short of a miracle!

147

'Asymmetric' means the line is imbalanced in favour of receiving data – with ADSL it is possible to receive at more than 6 Kbps but outbound transmission is limited to around 64 Kbps. As most home connections surf the web and download files, video and music, ADSL is ideally suited for this purpose. However, if a web server was connected or an organisation made large and frequent transmissions, ADSL would not be so suitable. There would be a considerable difference in speed when downloading a file compared to uploading.

DSL technology has been a godsend to the telephone companies. It has allowed them to provide high bandwidth data rates to dispersed locations with relatively small changes to the existing telephone infrastructure. DSL technologies seem likely to develop in the coming decade, delivering an even higher bandwidth – VDSL (Very High Data Rate DSL) should become common, enabling 55 Mbps to the home.

Cable modems

Many parts of the country have now been provided with Internet access through cable TV systems. In most parts of the UK, the cable systems that have been installed have been designed to transfer data, and it is common to find integrated cable modems inside cable TV boxes. Again, using Frequency Division Multiplexing (FDM), data is effectively added to the cable system using a separate, dedicated frequency. However, because the cable is under the control of the cable company and has a much greater bandwidth than twisted pair, cable companies are able to tailor their service and to offer higher data rates than ADSL. For example, most cable companies can offer at least a 1 Mb connection and they can tailor its direction – a residential customer is more likely to download information than to upload and so the cable company will provide a faster downstream connection than upstream. A web-hosting company would probably want the connection the other way around.

Like DSL, cable modems provide a permanent connection to the Internet: they are always on, and when the computer is on, they can represent a security hazard. Usually, the frequency used by the cable companies is employed to provide an extended ethernet network over a WAN, with a geographical reach of up to 100 miles. It is therefore not unusual to see a cable box with a dedicated ethernet port at the rear.

ISDN

Integrated Services Digital Network (ISDN) was and still is very popular in the USA but never really caught on in the UK, largely due to price. With ISDN, a telephone subscriber is provided with two digital telephone lines. If they are used for voice, they require special telephones to be connected to them. The most common ISDN connection is ISDN2, which provides two bearer (or B) channels each of which can carry 64 Kbps and one Delta (or D) channel that establishes and manages the session. Thus ISDN provides a maximum of 128 Kbps in either direction. This must, of course, be matched by the ISP. The subscriber pays call costs for ISDN and also for the line rental for each of the lines. Thus a one-hour Internet session will cost twice as much as a one hour phone call and along with the rental for the two lines, this makes it very expensive when compared to ADSL.

ISDN is now mainly used for video conferencing and for large organisations that require an infrequently used backup line for WAN connections. ISDN is usually available as ISDN2, ISDN6 and ISDN30. The number represents the number of lines and hence the bearer channels. Thus for ISDN30 there are 30 lines, thirty 64 Kbps channels, thirty line rental charges to pay and thirty times the call costs. ISDN in the USA is slightly different from that in the UK and most of Europe.

Satellite

In early 2003, two companies began offering broadband connection speeds through a combination of satellite and telephone technology (Figure 11.2). Although this method has been available for some time, it is the use of the Sky Digital satellite system that makes this an affordable option – previously it was via a dedicated satellite.

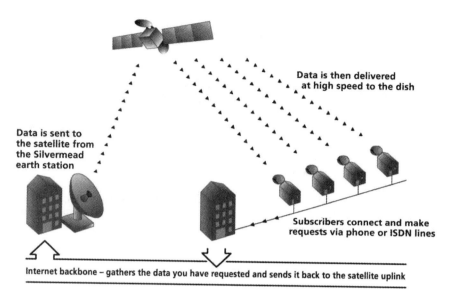

Figure 11.2   Broadband via satellite (courtesy of Silvermead)

This type of technology is probably most suitable for those who can't receive broadband services because of their location – remember, ADSL requires technology to be added to telephone exchanges, which could take quite some time in rural areas. Also, in some inner-city areas, subscribers are too far from their exchange to have ADSL. As shown in Figure 11.2, this technology uses the existing telephone line to send a request, say, for a web page to the ISP. The ISP then retrieves the page from the Internet at high speed and returns it via the satellite to the user. This should happen as quickly as conventional broadband services. The technology requires a satellite modem and a modification to a conventional satellite receiver. The main disadvantage of this technology is that it ties up a conventional telephone line. Other than that, as a service it is virtually identical to broadband – around 64 Kbps outbound and around 0.5 Mbps inbound.

Private wire

Organisations such as web-hosting companies, large institutions, e-commerce sites and universities that require very high-speed connection to the Internet can connect using private wires. These are private dedicated connections from the organisation to its ISP usually using fibre optic cabling. Using technologies such as ATM (see Chapter 5), this link can be as high as 155 Mbps (providing the receiving ISP can handle it) but it is expensive.

─── CRUCIAL TIP ───

It is important you understand the various connections to the Internet and their characteristics. You will almost certainly be asked about this in an assessment.

CRUCIAL CONCEPT

Different types of Internet connection have different attributes. When deciding on a connection, the one that best matches the client's requirements should be chosen. Of course, it is important to make sure their ISP can handle it.

Quick test

Briefly discuss the major ways of connecting to the Internet.

Section 2

The Internet (TCP/IP) case study

Throughout this book, standards, equipment, topologies and technologies have been discussed. Whilst understanding all this is of crucial importance, we still have not considered the 'big picture' – i.e. how does it all work? If, for example, an ethernet or cable modem was chosen, how would the web browser download the information from the Internet? How does it find the information?

This section intends to answer these questions by outlining the process of connecting to the Internet and retrieving a web page. This section assumes an ethernet network connection is being used. If a modem is being used a serial link is simply being employed that connects to the ISP's LAN – it looks exactly the same except the connection to the PC from the LAN is serial.

Your Internet settings

Every computer connected to the Internet needs a minimum of three settings: an IP address, a subnet mask and a default gateway. These can be obtained either by going into the network settings from the control panel or by running the winipcfg command (Windows 98) or the ipconfig command (Windows NT, 2000 and XP). Figure 11.3 shows sample output from the winipcfg command.

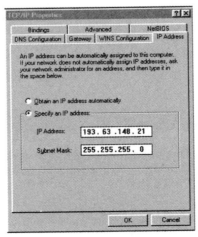

Figure 11.3 Ethernet settings (networking option from control panel in Windows 98)

Looking at each of the settings in turn, the adaptor address is the MAC address of the ethernet NIC (see Chapter 5). The IP address is the computer's logical address on the Internet (see Chapter 3) and the subnet mask is a binary pattern used to locate the network. The default gateway is the place to which the computer sends the packet if it has no idea what else to do with it.

In the IP address, the first byte tells us that this is a class C address (because it is in the class C address range – see Chapter 3). Thus the first three bytes are used to specify the network address (in this case 193.63.148). The subnet mask (see Chapter 3) 255.255.255.0 tells us to compare the first three bytes to determine the subnetwork. Thus we can see that the default gateway is on the same subnetwork as the machine itself (because the first three bytes are identical). An address of 18.98.38.1 would be on a different subnet.

However, how does this relate to a web page? A URL is essentially a text representation of an IP address. When we enter a URL (e.g. osiris.sunderland.ac.uk) into a web browser, the web browser communicates with a domain name server (DNS) and retrieves the IP address but it doesn't display it. So if 157.228.102.1 is keyed into your browser, it will retrieve the same page as if osiris.sunderland.ac.uk had been keyed in. To locate the DNS server, the machine broadcasts an Ethernet frame that looks for a DNS server.

─CRUCIAL TIP─

Examine the settings on your PC and then try keying 157.228.102.1 into your browser.

Beginning the journey

Figure 11.4 represents an Internet connection.

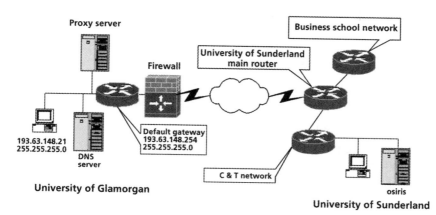

Figure 11.4   An Internet connection

A PC at the University of Glamorgan is being used to view the home page of the School of Computing and Technology at the University of Sunderland (osiris.sunderland.ac.uk). Both networks are ethernet. The URL is entered into the browser, which immediately queries the DNS server and retrieves the IP address of 157.228.102.1. It does this by broadcasting an ethernet frame to the DNS server which then responds with a unicast frame (to one machine only) containing the IP address. For our purposes it does not matter how the DNS server knows the address – very crudely, all DNSs across the world talk to one another to update their tables.

The machine at Glamorgan now knows the address of osiris.sunderland.ac.uk as 157.228.102.1. It uses its subnet mask to identify the parts of the address that give the network address (see Chapter 3). It does this by logic: by ANDing the address and the subnet mask together. In binary 255 is 11111111 – all bits are 1 in the byte. A bit set to 1 means compare. Thus 255.255.255.0 means compare all parts of the first three bytes. The network portion of the IP address is therefore 193.63.148 (the last byte is the host ID – the Glamorgan PC in this case). As 193.63.148 and 157.228.102 are not identical The PC knows the machine it is looking for is not on the same network as itself.

CRUCIAL CONCEPT

This very brief description of subnetworking (or subnetting) is fundamental to networking and the Internet. Networks are divided to lessen the load on them. In Chapter 6 we saw that a bridge or switch can help control collisions but they can't control broadcasts – routers and subnets are needed for this. (More information on subnetting is contained in Chapter 3.)

The Glamorgan machine does not know what to do with the packet. However, it has been programmed to send such packets to the default gateway. Although the PC knows the IP address of the default gateway, it has no idea of the MAC address of the default gateway. To find the MAC address, it needs to resolve the IP address. It does this through a process known as address resolution protocol (ARP). The machine broadcasts an ethernet frame which asks the machine that has the IP address of 193.63.148.254 to respond with its MAC address. The default gateway router receives this broadcast and realises the IP address is its own. It then responds with a unicast frame to the Glamorgan PC. It can unicast because it knows the Glamorgan PC's MAC address – it was in its frame – and, obviously, it knows its own address. Unicasts are preferable to broadcasts as they do not consume as much network bandwidth (they go to one machine only, not all the machines).

CRUCIAL TIP

After accessing a web page, key in arp -a at your command prompt. You will see the ARP cache – a map of IP and MAC addresses.

The Glamorgan PC now knows the MAC address of the default gateway, and it encapsulates the IP packet requesting the web page into an Ethernet frame addressed to the default gateway. This frame is placed on to the Ethernet network where it begins its journey to the default gateway.

The proxy server

In the event the University of Glamorgan uses a proxy server, the browser will itself request that the IP address of the requested web page is sent to the proxy. It does this for two reasons. The first is to establish if the proxy already holds a copy of that web page. It if does, it can retrieve it more quickly and less expensively than if it went to the Internet (ISPs and directly connected companies are charged for the use of certain links – e.g. Transatlantic). Secondly, it checks the organisation's security policy – is this URL allowed? The proxy server then handles the retrieval of the web page itself, sending it to the default gateway.

The default gateway

If the proxy server and/or the PC don't know the whereabouts of a web page, the request lands at the default gateway. The default gateway is usually a router and it may have a number of routes connected to it. As we saw in Chapter 6, routers have two purposes – to determine the best path and to switch the packet. In this case, the router needs to determine which of the paths it is directly connected to will lead to the required IP address. It isn't feasible for a router to know every IP address on the Internet and so it, too, has a default gateway: if it doesn't know what to do with a packet it forwards it to its default gateway.

In our example, the University of Glamorgan router is connected only to the Internet and the Glamorgan network. As a 157.228.102 address clearly doesn't belong to the University of Glamorgan, the router has no idea what to do with it and so sends it to its default gateway – in this case, on to the Internet.

Firewall

Before passing on to the Internet, the packet may be subjected to a firewall. A firewall is a piece of software whose purpose is to provide greater network security. A firewall can be thought of as a collection of numbered, and guarded exit doors to an organisation: employees have to leave by certain numbered doors and, if the doors are locked (perhaps it's not time for them to leave), they can't get out. If the door is unlocked, they can leave but they may be subjected to a search to determine if they are carrying any secrets.

A firewall does exactly the same thing with data. Data exiting from an organisation does so via port numbers (the door numbers in the analogy), which can be open or closed. Commonly used port numbers are:

Port	Application
21	FTP
23	Telnet
25	SMTP
80	Web.

Packets passing through the firewall may also be subjected to a search to see if they contain any data that isn't allowed under the organisation's security policy. If they do, they are dealt with severely – they are destroyed!

CRUCIAL CONCEPT

Firewalls are an important part of an organisation's security but they aren't all an organisation needs – they should be part of a policy that includes routers and proxy servers. The policy should also recognise network users. Without such an integrated policy, firewalls are of little use.

On to the Internet

If packets pass successfully through the firewall, they are ready to be placed on to the Internet. Almost certainly, the bandwidth of the organisation's Internet connection will be smaller than that of its LAN. Not all packets will be able to fit on to such a limited bandwidth and so some will be lost. TCP (transmission control protocol – see Chapter 4) waits for an acknowledgement from the recipient of the packets transmitted. In the event it does not receive one, it simply sends a replacement packet. Once on the Internet, the packets head toward huge routers with huge routing tables. When they arrive at these routers, their destination IP address is examined and, if the router knows the route the packet should take, it is switched to that route. If not, it is forwarded to that router's default gateway.

Often represented as a cloud (as in Figure 11.4), the Internet is a complex web of connections and routers. However, one thing that should be noted about the Internet is that it operates on TCP that is inherently reliable. As the Internet is such a mass of connections, each has several backups. For example, there are satellite connections between the UK and the USA but there are also trans-oceanic cables and satellite connections to and from Europe to the USA. Thus a transmission will almost always get through even if links are down – the Internet will route around the downed links. The reliability of the Internet was harrowingly demonstrated on 11 September 2001. After the aircraft hit the World Trade Center, all conventional telephone services were lost. However, IP telephones (operating via the Internet) were able to route around the downed links.

Arriving at the destination

Eventually the packet will approach the University of Sunderland and will arrive at its router. When it arrives, it will be immediately subjected to a firewall. If it is bound for an open door, it will be allowed. If not, it will simply be destroyed. Once through the door, it will be inspected by the firewall to determine if it is the sort of packet that should be allowed through. Providing it is, it is passed on to the university LAN (encapsulated in an ethernet frame). After the firewall, a router, will examine the network element of the IP address and forward the packet to the appropriate network. Once it arrives on the appropriate network, the router on that network will either know the MAC address of osiris or it will ARP to get it. Once it has the MAC address of osiris, it will forward the IP packet (inside an ethernet frame) to osiris. Osiris will open the packet and examine the contents – a request for a web page. Osiris will then recycle the packet, replacing the destination address with the source address (i.e. putting the address of the Glamorgan machine as the destination and its own address as the source).

The return journey

If the contents of the web page are too large to fit into one packet, the server will replicate the packet structure and fill this with more data. It will then fill the packet with the required contents and send the packet back: to the default gateway, to the university proxy server, through the firewall and on to the Internet. Once it arrives at the University of Glamorgan, it will be subjected to the firewall and will then on to the university LAN. It will pass on to the proxy server (inside an ethernet frame because it's on a LAN), which will check its contents. If the proxy allows the packet through, it will take a copy of it so that further requests for that web page can be satisfied from it rather than having to go on to the Internet. It will then be passed to the router to be delivered to the machine.

As the router knows the MAC address of this machine, all this happens in the blink of an eye. The router encapsulates the packet inside a frame and sends it to the machine. The machine strips off the ethernet and IP headers, extracts the data and displays it.

Summary

In this discussion of the Internet and of how networks (in this case the ethernet) facilitate the movement of traffic to and from the Internet, only the most important networking device – the router – has been highlighted. Typically, however, ethernet frames would pass through a host of ethernet networking devices, including switches and hubs.

--- CRUCIAL CONCEPT ---

Packets contains web page requests travel far – across ethernet networks and the Internet and through many, varied devices.

Quick test

Briefly outline how a request for a web page generates both ethernet frames and IP packets and how these result in the web page being retrieved and displayed.

Section 3

End of chapter assessment

Questions

1. Identify the most common ways of connecting a home PC to the Internet. Briefly discuss each, highlighting their advantages and disadvantages.

2. Briefly outline how a request for a web page makes its way to the Internet.

Answers

1. To answer this question, you need to list the most popular connections from the home to the Internet (i.e modem access, DSL, cable and ISDN). For each of these connections, you need to discuss the features of the connection type – for example, always on, the equipment needed for the connection and the advantages and disadvantages. For instance, ADSL is asymmetric, which makes it ideal for connecting from the home: it has a faster downstream connection than upstream; there are no call costs; and it is faster than a conventional (modem) connection. You should also discuss the disadvantages – for example, it has a slower upload speed than download and, although still faster than a modem connection, it may not be suitable for all teleworking.

2. As you couldn't possibly discuss all that is covered in this chapter in an exam question, this question is only concerned with how a request for a web page makes its way from the PC to the Internet. In practice, networks are most likely to be ethernet, and so you should state this before you start. The best place to start is a discussion of the network settings on a PC and what they mean and do. From that you can expand your answer to discuss how the PC decides whether or not the web server is on the same network as the PC. Assuming it is, it will cut out most of the answer to the question and a good part of your marks! Therefore assume it isn't and show the role of the default gateway, default gateways set on the router, the proxy server and the firewall.

Section 4

Further reading and research

See the *www.PhilipIrving.com* web site for up-to-date further reading and support for this chapter.

Cisco Networking Academy Program (2001) *First Year Companion Guide* (2nd edn). Cisco Press. ISBN: 1 58713 025 4. Chapter 30.

Dick, D. (2002) *PC Support Handbook*. Dumbreck Publishing. ISBN: 0 95417 110 1. Data communications chapter.

Chapter 12
Revision

Chapter summary

This chapter is different from the others as it aims to help you achieve good marks in assignments and exams/TCTs. It contains a sample assignment and a sample time-constrained test, along with suggested worked solutions. These are based on real assignments and TCTs.

Section 1

How to tackle assignment questions

Introduction

Assessors are required to submit a marking scheme along with their assessment. To gain maximum marks from the assessment, you need to be able to discuss as many points on the marking scheme as possible. A common mistake in answering assessments is to avoid the more difficult parts – in doing so, you are giving up potential marks. Assignments often present scenarios and these appear complicated. Appearances can be deceptive: the assignment might be quite straightforward. The mark of a good consultant is being able to go into an organisation knowing the information he or she wants. He or she can often extract this information from the organisation even though the organisation itself cannot supply it.

In an assignment situation you are the consultant and need to extract the information not from an organisation but from a case study. Often the case study will have been deliberately created to cover most of the syllabus. What follows is an assignment similar to those used at the University of Sunderland. Although assignments will vary from one institution to another, it will serve as a guideline as to what the assessor is looking for in the answers you give.

Sample assignment

Introduction

Sir Philip Irving, a local businessman has helped to raise money for a special pensioners' project in a deprived area of a city. Grangetown Computing (GC) will specialise in short computer courses for the elderly. Sir Philip has raised enough money to cover the building of an IT suite, which will involve the installation of a network infrastructure as well as 100 PCs. The other money is to be provided by a grant.

Work has already commenced on the building, and the contractors estimate that they can begin installation of the network infrastructure within three months. The equipment must be purchased before this date with all invoices paid within one month, otherwise the grant will be lost. Unfortunately neither Sir Philip nor the contractors have any idea of what kind of networking infrastructure should be installed at the GC. It has therefore been decided that bids will be obtained from local companies to design, supply and supervise the installation of the networking infrastructure. Being wary of small companies, Sir Philip has contracted a local potential GC user, Mr Warrender, who has had some networking experience. Mr Warrender will have the task of reviewing rival bids to ensure these are appropriate for the centre's requirements. He must also ensure that the successful bidders provide a reasonable level of 'future proofing' and that the contractors understand the requirements and meet them through knowledge and good design rather than luck. Accordingly, Mr Warrender has set out a scoring mechanism against which the network contractors will be scored. The company that scores the highest points should have demonstrated better knowledge and design details and therefore will be recommended to Sir Philip for detailed contract negotiations.

Current equipment

GC plan to create three IT working areas – one for male pensioners, one for female pensioners and a larger common facility for mixed groups. Both the male and female IT areas will be equipped with 20 machines each. The larger common IT facility will be equipped with 100 machines.

Sir Philip has received 25 IBM token ring adaptor cards and 170 10Base2 network cards from a local benefactor and is keen these be used in the centre provided they do not add any cost to the overall project.

To make maximum use of the facilities, it has been determined that individual sessions will last for only one hour (starting at 9.00 am and finishing at 4.00 pm with one hour off for lunch), Monday to Friday. It is a contractual condition that users will be able to use any program within three minutes of starting up.

Mr Warrender has made an initial survey and has produced the following as a basis for the design:

Area	Program estimate (MB)	Data estimate (MB)	Print load/hour (MB)
Male area	6	10	10
Female area	5	4	8
Common area	13	6	12

All estimates are on a per machine basis.

As the costs for carrying out the work are unclear, Mr Warrender has decided to ask for two separate prices. To keep the cost of software down per machine, it has been decided that both the male and female areas will have their own dedicated servers and operate on a client/server basis. The common area will be similar but can make use of two servers to cut down network traffic. In the first bid cost, it is assumed that each network will be standalone with no interconnection between systems. Software costs will come from a different budget but all hardware costs must be accounted for – including the costs of servers.

In Mr Warrender's second scenario, he would like to see a fully integrated facility with email and Internet access to all computers. He has also specified that, for security reasons, all servers should be moved out of each area and placed in a common lockable area to be located on the ground floor. As part of a cost saving to help finance this enhanced facility, Mr Warrender has estimated that the number of servers could be reduced to three.

The server room (if used), as well as the common IT area, is to be located on the ground floor with both the male and female IT areas on the first floor. The first floor will also house another of Sir Philip's enterprises, Phil's Taxis. Unfortunately, the radios that will be used in this venture grossly exceed the normal transmission limits for this type of equipment.

The GC will use a converted 'listed' building that has solid floors and suspended ceilings. Under the terms of the lease, only one drop for cabling between floors will be permitted, somewhere close to the lift shaft. The planning department has also insisted that cabling from the female IT area must pass through Phil's Radio Taxis' room before dropping to the ground floor where the server is to be located.

As well as forming three distinct networks, in the second of the two proposals it has been determined that these networks should be linked to provide for local file exchange as well as to allow a single shared connection to the Internet (it has been estimated that this will require an overall capacity of 1 Mbps connection speed at peak times). Sir Philip has made it a requirement that bidders provide some way of preventing unsuitable materials from being accessed at this facility.

The layout of the building will be as follows:

Ground floor

Server room		Office
Lift	Common IT area	
		Reception area and stairway
	Canteen	

First floor

Male IT area	Phil's Radio Taxis	Female IT area
Lift	Corridor	Stairs
Toilets	Storage	

Requirements

Your task is to analyse the requirements of GC and to produce the following for submission:

1. A report detailing whether the networking cards donated by the local benefactor could be used in the overall scheme. (20%)

2. A detailed design of the basic scheme with costs. (20%)
3. A detailed design of the enhanced scheme including central servers, email and Internet access with costs. (20%)
4. A report confirming compatibility, together with sketches illustrating how each design will be implemented. (10%)
5. A report explaining how unsuitable material can be kept out of such facilities. (10%)
6. Detailed instructions concerning the installation of Linux, including creating users and groups. (20%)

Marking scheme

Question 1

As you will have probably guessed, this assignment requires capacity planning. The first step in this is to trawl the assignment looking for facts and figures. It is not uncommon for an assessor to start off with a relatively simple capacity plan and then to 'pad this out' with lots of useless information and red herrings. This gets you to search for the required information. A sample capacity plan follows:

Report on the possibility of using the existing networking cards

Male area	Program + Data	= 16 Mb
Total load at start	$20 \times 16 \times 8$	= 2560 Mbps
Loading time for 10Base2	2560/7 seconds	= 6.09 minutes
Loading time for TR	2560/16 seconds	= 2.67 minutes
Loading time for 100BaseT	2560/100 seconds	= 0.43 minutes
Female area	Program + data	= 9 Mb
Total load at start	$20 \times 9 \times 8$	= 1440 Mbps
Loading time for 10Base2	1440/7 seconds	= 3.43 minutes
Loading time for TR	1440/16 seconds	= 1.50 minutes
Loading time for 100BaseT	1440/100 seconds	= 0.24 minutes
Common area	Program + data	= 19 Mb
Assume two distinct networks, then		
total load at start	$50 \times 19 \times 8$	= 7600 Mbps
Loading time for 10Base2	7600/7 seconds	= 18.10 minutes
Loading time for TR	7600/16 seconds	= 7.92 minutes
Loading time for 100BaseT	7600/100 seconds	= 1.27 minutes

Note that none of the above times include any contingency allowance.

All 10Base2 cards can be ruled out on start-up performance.

Although token ring cards could be used in either the male or female areas, it should be noted that there are insufficient cards for both rooms. Therefore use in the female area could be considered but more than likely ruled out on the basis of standardisation and the costs to replace. (20%)

CRUCIAL TIP

It is very, very important to show your workings out. You will receive more marks for the process than you do for the correct result. You will, of course, receive maximum marks if you get both right! However, if you go off track the assessor will usually give you marks if the process is right.

Question 2

In the initial scenario, there should be four distinct networks with four servers. Each network will be 100BaseT ethernet (except possibly the female area) as described above.

Calculations and design to be given plus costs. (20%)

> ──────────────── CRUCIAL TIP ────────────────
>
> Capacity planning again – the assessor is asking you to demonstrate that your network will work. As you now know, there is far more to networking that simply plugging two machines together.

Question 3

In the second scenario, we can combine the server for the male and female areas. Cables from the female area passing through Phil's Radio Taxis will be subject to interference from the high output radio and should be fibre – most likely 100BaseF using media converters (include the costs). (20%)

> ──────────────── CRUCIAL TIP ────────────────
>
> Don't just give a list of equipment and prices. If you were spending many thousands of pounds you wouldn't just expect a shopping list: you would expect some sort of justification, and you must provide this justification for marks. Anyone can throw together a shopping list but, if you want good marks, justify each item, discuss alternatives and outline why you made the choice. For example, to those unfamiliar with networking, there would seem no point in using fibre in the taxi room.

Question 4

In this part, the assessor is asking you to demonstrate that you have confidence your design and selected equipment will work. You can do this by supplying catalogue cuttings that show the equipment and their technical specifications. You should annotate these with details of which interfaces, etc., you are going to use and how these will connect. (20%)

> ──────────────── CRUCIAL TIP ────────────────
>
> The assessor is asking you to prove that you didn't take a pin and stick it randomly in a catalogue to come up with the equipment. The assessor is asking you to demonstrate that the kit is compatible and that you have made sure it will link. You may have to justify your choices.

Question 5

There are controls in Internet Explorer and also in such products as Netnanny that can help restrict access to the Internet. However, such restrictions should really be formalised and implemented through an organisational security policy. In particular, they should be implemented using proxies, firewalls and routers. (20%)

> ──────────────── CRUCIAL TIP ────────────────
>
> The assessor is asking you to think as a network professional and expects you to go for an organisational-level solution to the problem. Choosing Netnanny is a PC-level solution.

Question 6

Your report should detail how Linux is installed and also how to create users and groups. (20%)

> ──────────────── CRUCIAL TIP ────────────────
>
> As mentioned elsewhere, assessors now find it difficult to watch students build Linux machines. One solution is to ask you to produce a manual that will assist someone else to install Linux. This is what you are being asked for: a step-by-step guide for installing Linux, creating users and groups and allocating users to groups.

Section 2

How to tackle exam questions

Introduction

As noted earlier, assessors are required to submit a marking scheme along with their exam/ TCT questions. To gain maximum marks from the exam/TCT you need to be able to discuss as many points on the marking scheme as possible. Simply writing something about the subject will gain you very few marks – ensure you know enough about the question to make it worth your while answering it.

Exams or time constrained tests have, as their name suggests, time restrictions, and will often ask specific questions rather than give you a scenario. The assessor is looking to test your knowledge. Contrary to popular belief, exams/TCTs are not there to fail you: they are for assessment integrity purposes. For this reason they are often treated as a true representation of your abilities – make sure you do yourself justice!

What follows are TCTs similar to those used at the University of Sunderland. Although TCTs/ exams will vary from one institution to another, they will serve as a guideline to what the assessor is looking for in the answers you give.

Sample TCT – rubric

CRUCIAL TIP

Read the rubric! The rubric is the rules of the TCT/exam. It is the part at the front that gives you information about which questions you should attempt, what marks they carry, how many you should attempt and whether calculators or books can be used.

It is a common mistake to arrive at an exam and 'jump straight in'. Imagine how you would feel if you did just that with a capacity planning question: you did not use a calculator but found afterwards your fellow students did!

This TCT consists of three sections. The questions in section A are multiple choice – the correct answer should be ringed. Section B and C questions are written answer questions.

Section A questions are worth 4 marks (correct) or −1 mark (incorrect) (10 questions). If no answer is given, you neither receive a mark nor lose a mark. There is only one correct answer to each question.

Section B questions are worth 30 marks each (one question to be attempted).

The Section C question is worth 30 marks (compulsory).

CRUCIAL TIP

This is a kind assessor – you are being given a pass (40%) just for the multiple-choice questions. If you have revised this should be easy!

Sample TCT: multiple choice questions

Section A

1. Which of the following does not adversely influence communication on a network?

    a) attenuation
    b) impulse noise
    c) bandwidth increase
    d) intermodulation
    e) crosstalk

2. What is the function of a modem?

    a) to boost the signal strength
    b) to allow a computer to be connected to an RS232C line
    c) to allow data to be sent over a telephone line
    d) to allow connection to a token ring network
    e) to allow an RS232C line to run over a much greater distance

3. Which of the following cables would be used to connect to a 10BaseT network system?

    a) fibre optic cable
    b) MICC cable
    c) coaxial cable
    d) printer cable
    e) CAT 5/UTP cable

4. On what topology does FDDI operate?

    a) star
    b) ring
    c) bus
    d) tree
    e) point-to-point

5. The following is a brief description of one of the layers in the ISO seven-layer model for open system interconnection: 'converts data into an abstract format ... compresses data... associated with file types such as JPEG, GIF, etc.' Which of the following layers fits the description?

    a) physical
    b) presentation
    c) network
    d) transport
    e) session

6. Which ISO seven-layers would be used by a bridge?

    a) physical only
    b) physical + data link layer
    c) physical + data link + network layer
    d) physical + data link + network + transport layer
    e) physical + data link + network + transport + session layer

7. Which command is important for file system security in UNIX?

    a) security
    b) chmod
    c) modify

d) delete
e) lock

8. Which command is useful for establishing inherited rights in UNIX?

    a) umask
    b) mark
    c) mask
    d) rights
    e) lefts

9. What is the following a definition of? 'This category of networks usually spans a university campus or, at its limits, a small geographical area – for example, a town, county or district.':

    a) LAN
    b) WAN
    c) MAN
    d) district
    e) region

10. Which of the following is **not** a layer in the TCP/IP model?

    a) network access
    b) internetwork
    c) application
    d) transport
    e) presentation

Section B
Answer **one question** out of the following:

1. Networks commonly use the following components:

    a) repeaters
    b) bridges
    c) routers
    d) gateways.

    Describe the purpose **of two only** of these components, showing clearly how these can be used within a network. (15 marks each)

2. Local area networks are generally interconnected using either copper or fibre optic cables. With the aid of a diagram, describe the construction of the following cables clearly stating where each type would typically be used:

    - Coaxial cable (5 and 10 mm)   (5 marks)
    - STP cable   (5 marks)
    - UTP cable   (5 marks)
    - Fibre optic cable   (5 marks).

    Show how data is carried in a fibre optic cable and explain the main advantages of using this type of medium. (10 marks)

3. The ethernet is a widely used technology for local area networks (LANs):

    a) Describe in detail the operation of the ethernet and list the supported topologies. (15 marks)
    b) Compare the advantages and disadvantages of the ethernet with those of another

popular networking technology. (15 marks)

Section C

Answer the following question:

1. There are essentially three types of backup:

   - Name the three types. (6 marks)
   - Discuss each type and compare its advantages/disadvantages compared to the others. (24 marks)

Sample TCT: multiple choice questions

Section A answers

CRUCIAL TIP

Look for the red herrings! In general, multiple choice answers contain two answers that are 'possibles' and some that are red herrings. Look for the red herrings and eliminate them.

1. Answer c (bandwidth increase) – all the rest are legitimate sources of error!
2. Answer c (to allow data to be sent over a telephone line) – modems modulate digital-to-analogue signals and vice versa; they are needed to send data over a telephone line.
3. Answer e (CAT 5/UTP Cable) – 10BaseT uses twisted pair in a star configuration and the T stands for twisted pair!
4. Answer b (ring) – FDDI is similar to token ring and operates on a dual concentric fibre ring.
5. Answer b (presentation) – these functions are associated with the presentation layer.
6. Answer b (physical + data link layer) – a bridge operates in layer 2 and therefore uses the services of layer 1.
7. Answer b (chmod) – the chmod command modifies file attributes – the primary file security in UNIX.
8. Answer a (umask) – this specifies the default file creation mask – remember its rights taken away!
9. Answer c (MAN) – the town, regional or university campus should give this away.
10. Answer e (presentation) – remember ATIN!

Section B answers

Question 1
- Repeater: A device used to regenerate digital signals in both directions. It is used to extend the maximum size of a network (either in terms of numbers of nodes and/or operating distance). Operates on the OSI layer 1 (physical layer) and thus requires little intelligence.
- Bridge: A device used for three reasons – to:

   1. interconnect two smaller networks when the combined size exceeds the physical limitations of that technology. Communication can take place through the bridge;
   2. manage traffic and security between two separate networks only allowing internetwork traffic to pass through the bridge and thus ensuring that traffic local to one network does not cross to the other network;
   3. provide a conversion between technologies.

   Operates on OSI layer 2 (data link layer)

- Router: This is a device used to interconnect networks that are administratively separate or of a different network topology. These operate on OSI layer 3 (network layer) and are commonly used to connect a network to the Internet. They require no knowledge of the network to which they are connecting.

- Gateway: This is a device used to interconnect systems with different network protocols. This operates on OSI layer 7 (application layer). An example would be the exchange of email between two computers in different networks using a mail gateway.

Question 2

- 5 and 10 mm coaxial cable:

Plastic jacket — Braided metal shielding — Polyethylene dielectric — Centre conductor

You should discuss the fact that 5 mm coaxial cable is employed in 10Base2 ethernet systems primarily used in small office and workplace environments where distance is not a major concern. Also that 5 mm coaxial is reasonably flexible and can be hidden easily. On the other hand, 10 mm coaxial cable is used in 10Base5 ethernet systems where more distance is required. It is not particularly flexible and, hence, not easy to hide as it requires a significant turning radius, etc.

- STP cable:

Screen twisted pair cable is used in 10BaseT and 100BaseT ethernet environments. You should mention that the screened version of this cable gives better noise immunity but is more expensive and is more difficult to install due to the larger bending radius.

- UTP cable:

Unshielded twisted pair cable is used in 10BaseT and 100BaseT ethernet environments. You should discuss the fact that it is essentially the same as telephone cables and is often used in home and small office environments where cables can be hidden very easily and where noise is not a significant issue.

- Fibre optic cable:

Sheath — Individual fibre jacket — Cladding — Optical fibre — Reinforcing material

You should discuss the fact that fibre optic cable is more expensive than its copper counterparts and is used in high data rate transfer situations, such as FDDI and gigabit technologies. It is also used in areas susceptible to electrical noise due to its natural immunity. You should also note that fibre optic cable must tolerate large bending radii.

165

The following are the things you should discuss. Fibre optic cable consists of strands of optical fibres (traditionally, glass or some form of plastic equivalent) packaged within a protected environment similar to normal cable construction. Each fibre represents a communication channel. Light pulses pass longitudinally down the fibre to a receiving station where the original electrical signals can be regenerated. The fibre acts as a light tube reflecting the beam on its inner surface, which ensures there are very low losses of light over distance. Fibre optics, therefore, have a very high bandwidth compared to copper cables and, as they have very low losses, they can operate over very long distances. Being light pulses, the signals are completely immune to any form of electromagnetic radiation and, hence, immune to electrical noise.

Question 3: You should explain how data is sent across an ethernet network, including waiting for a transmission pause; reading back the data being transmitted to ensure no collisions have taken place; and dealing with collisions. The topologies supported include bus, tree and star. Ideally your comparison should be made with token ring as this is also a LAN technology. Its advantages include cost and ease of implementation. Its disadvantages include its performance under high loads (collisions), its relatively short range and the need for some form of repeaters even if only a small number of devices are connected to the network.

Section C answer

Full, differential and incremental.
You need to discuss each type of backup and the advantages and disadvantages of each. Full backup is the recommended method.

CRUCIAL TIP

You will earn marks simply for naming the different types of backup, so you may as well have them. In the second part, the assessor wants you to show you understand the different types and can discuss these professionally, identifying the advantages and disadvantages of each.

Glossary

ADSL Asymmetric digital subscriber line.

ASCII American Standard Code for Information Interchange.

backbone (cabling) This is the cabling that connects the main network components – for example, switches, routers, etc. It forms the backbone of the network.

baud Measure of the number of times a signal varies per second. Often confused with bits per second as early systems encoded one bit per signal variation. Modern systems encode multiple bits on a signal variation.

bit Binary digIT, a 1 or a 0 – the basic level at which computers operate.

bps Bits per second – a measure of throughput usually related to networks. The number of bits per second that can be/are transferred.

Cat 3 Telephone cable that cannot handle high-speed data. Techniques can be used to improve performance, such as ADSL.

Cat 5 This is the most common form of cabling in networking. Most new buildings are wired using this cable. It is capable of handling data transmission at 100 Mbps.

CRC Cyclic redundancy check – an error-detection mechanism.

DNS Domain name server – this is the network server that converts the URL into an IP number.

EISA Extended industry standard architecture – a popular architecture used in computers in the 1990s.

flow control The ability to restrict the flow of information to accommodate slower devices on the network.

FTP file transfer protocol – used to send files across a computer network.

Gbps Gigabits per second (1000 Mbps).

HTTP Hyper text transfer protocol – used to transfer web pages across a network.

IP Internet protocol – the networking protocol that is used on the Internet.

IP number In version 4, a 4-byte dotted decimal number (e.g. 157.228.102.1) which represents the logical address of a computer on the Internet.

ISA Industry standard architecture – the first internal PC architecture used by IBM-compatible PCs.

MB Megabits

MB Megabytes – different from megabits.

Mbps Megabits per second – different from megabytes. Also written as Mbit/s.

MCA Micro channel architecture – an internal PC architecture developed by IBM for its PS/2 and RS6000 range of computers.

NIC Network interface card.

NOS Networked operating system (e.g. Novell).

Parity An error-detection mechanism – a bit is added to the end of a series of bits (usually a byte) to permit an error in the transmission to be detected.

PCI Peripheral component interconnect – an Intel-devised internal computer architecture that provides much greater speeds than either ISA or EISA.

PCMCIA The architecture used by laptops and other small devices – credit card-sized interface cards.

SMTP Simple mail transfer protocol – used by mail servers to exchange email.

STP Shielded twisted pair cabling – more immune to interference than UTP.

TCP Transmission control protocol – the transmission control method used by the Internet.

TFTP Trivial file transfer protocol – used for small files. Less reliable than FTP.

URL Uniform resource locator – a web address (e.g. cisco.sunderland.ac.uk).

USB Universal serial bus – a high-speed serial interface.

USB2 A faster version of USB.

UTP Unshielded twisted pair cabling – widely used in modern installations.

VLAN Virtual LAN – a protocol enabling a LAN to be divided into several virtual LANs.

VPN Virtual private network – a protocol for establishing (virtual) private networks over the Internet.

WiFi Same as WLAN

WLAN Wireless local area network – a wire-free networking solution.

Index